Studies on Asia
1961

Studies on Asia, 1961 is Volume II in the series.

STUDIES ON ASIA, 1961

ROBERT K. SAKAI
Editor

- **ROBERT I. CRANE**
  University of Michigan

- **MINOO ADENWALLA**
  Lawrence College

- **PHILIP S. THOMAS**
  Grinnell College

- **RALPH M. MIWA**
  University of Missouri

- **MANUEL SARKISYANZ**
  Universities of Kiel and Freiburg

- **FRED R. VON DER MEHDEN**
  University of Wisconsin

- **RICHARD BUTWELL**
  University of Illinois

University of Nebraska Press
Lincoln
1961

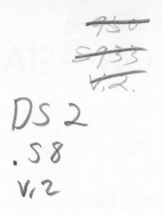

Publishers on the Plains

UNP

Contents

Contents

Introduction

Burma and India, two of the earlier nations to gain their independence in the post-World War II period, are now in the second decade of modern nationhood. It is appropriate that most of the papers in this second volume of *Studies on Asia* should deal with these two countries which have succeeded remarkably well in maintaining democratic processes of government despite severe stresses and strains. During the difficult initial years of national sovereignty, continuity and stability have been provided by the leaders of the independence movement who continued in positions of power largely by virtue of their prestige and popularity. The people of these countries now are in a position to assess their recent experiences with some deliberateness.

The second decade of nationhood may witness a gradual shift of power to a new generation of leaders whose major concern will be national reconstruction rather than revolution. In the process of reconstruction there already have developed rival claims of regionalism, of class interests, of traditionalism versus modernism. These conflicts will influence the development of democracy, the political structure of the nation, the nature of the economic system, and the national educational policies.

It is timely, therefore, that several of the authors in this volume have suggested the need for new approaches and reappraisals in the study of Asian societies. Professors Crane, Miwa, and Sarkisyanz are concerned that contemporary interpretations of Indian nationalism, Japanese imperialism, and Burmese socialism respectively are often imprecise, inadequate, and at times misleading. Coincident with the thesis presented by Professor Crane on divergent nationalisms in India is the recent warning sounded by Prime Minister Nehru that one of the gravest dangers to India today is "regional nationalism."

In his analysis of the ideology of Japanese imperialism, Professor Miwa denies that it was simply the product of aberrant minds. Though the theorists used proto-Marxian terms to denounce Western imperialism in order, paradoxically, to justify Japanese aggrandizement, the arguments of these ultranationalists did have a certain consistency with the economic facts. Miwa seeks to explain the factors which made the rationale of Japanese imperialism plausible and acceptable to the prewar Japanese. The unstated implicit question he raises is whether or not the historic conditions he describes have been altered substantially in the present period.

Professor Thomas examines the prevailing economic views regarding a fundamental question in contemporary India, namely, how is she to use her limited capital resources for the maximum benefit of the country? After demonstrating the virtual impossibility of applying an economic yardstick to measure some of the social benefits of capital investment, he proposes his own formula which seeks to take into account such intangible derivatives. His method of analysis has the merit of keeping in the foreground the needs of the individual, which in a democratic society must not be submerged for the good of the total society.

The account which Professor Adenwalla has given on the influence of Hindu concepts in the Indian nationalist movement not only complements Crane's study, but also provides an interesting comparison with Sarkisyanz' analysis of Buddhist underpinnings for Burmese socialism. Both Adenwalla and Sarkisyanz show that there are bridges which link such modern movements as nationalism and socialism with the cultural traditions of these Asian societies.

The emphasis which Professor Von der Mehden has given to his description of Burmese politics stands in contrast to that of Sarkisyanz. The two essays bring out the issue of the significance of Buddhism in the contemporary life of Burma. It appears that no definitive answer can be given as yet. Another aspect of Buddhist politics, which is treated by Professor Butwell, is that of the rivalry between the military and the civilian groups. This poses for the Burmese an intriguing choice between the army's efficiency and U Nu's popularity and affinity for traditional symbols. Here again, the studies of Von der Mehden and Sarkisyanz lend depth to Butwell's report.

Each of the papers in this volume is exploratory in nature. They suggest the vast opportunities for research which exist in an area of the world where the past and the present have come into bewildering conjunction. With one exception, the papers were originally presented at the Ninth Annual Conference on Asian Affairs which met at the University of Oklahoma, October 28-29, 1960. Professor Thomas' paper was first presented at the Seventh Conference which convened at the University of Missouri. It is hoped that the publication of these articles, selected for their excellence, will promote the general objectives of the Conference of stimulating scholarly research, disseminating the results thereof, and broadening the area of understanding of Asian affairs.

ROBERT K. SAKAI

Problems of Divergent Developments within Indian Nationalism, 1895-1905

ROBERT I. CRANE

University of Michigan

There exists a body of literature which seeks to describe, in rather general terms, the development of nationalism in modern India. The main outlines of political nationalism have been reported, despite certain noteworthy gaps, so that the basic features are visible. Unfortunately, the bulk of the literature has been descriptive and, too often, polemic, rather than analytic and objective. Moreover, attention has been focussed too largely on the Congress Party—seen as a homogeneous or even monolithic structure—and too exclusively at the all-India level. At least two results can by now be noted. First, Indian nationalism has been depicted through a series of generalizations which, though acceptable at one level of explanation, leave a great deal to be desired in terms of depth and precision of interpretation. Second, a host of interesting and important qualifications—in detail—of the over-all situation have been ignored or have remained undiscovered. In short, the picture which emerges from the literature poses as many questions as it answers.[1]

Several factors contribute to the inadequacy of the present picture. One of these is the tendency to equate nationalism in India with the nationalism of the Western world in a manner which is both facile and misleading; another is the treatment of Indian nationalism as though it were one and the same thing in all parts of the subcontinent, at all periods of time, and for all classes of Indians. For our purposes, more serious is the tendency to study nationalism for itself, with little or no attempt to analyze its social, cultural, and economic origins or to get at the

1

social changes which have helped to create nationalism. These approaches are simplistic and tend to distort understanding of the dynamics of development of nationalism as a complex social, political, and intellectual process through time.[2]

In view of these considerations, it seems advisable to retrace our steps and analyze the growth of nationalism in India so as to account for real and significant divergencies. Such divergencies must be understood if a more accurate and effective concept is to emerge. In this brief paper an attempt will be made to suggest some of the more important divergencies within Indian nationalism and to indicate what their implications for analysis of nationalist growth may be. The focus of analysis will be the underlying social change which has taken place in India in recent decades and which is so crucial to an understanding of the contemporary Indian scene or an understanding of Indian nationalism.

Before discussing the major developmental variations within Indian nationalism, it would seem wise to present an initial definition of nationalism in the subcontinent so we may have an agreed-upon framework for further comment. The proposed definition is as follows:

> The nationalist movement in India developed as a response to European contact and domination. This is true in the sense that European education helped to create many of the core ideas of nationalism and in the sense that European rule served to create a number of the preconditions necessary for the growth of national sentiment. Moreover, alien domination produced a reaction amongst Indians regarding those aspects of foreign control which were felt to be intolerable. From this it may be argued that the nationalist leadership—serving as a kind of epitome of Indian response to Europeanization—sought to express or to represent the Indian reaction in such a way as to unite Indian opinion, mobilze public sentiment, formulate popular demands and state nationalist goals and objectives.[3]

In this definition an effort is made to stress the development of nationalism as a *response* to foreign ideas and foreign domination—a domination which brought about a number of changes in Indian society, in Indian thought, and in the traditional economy of the subcontinent. It should be noted, however, that foreign contact did not create *all* of the conditions necessary for a full-fledged and widespread Indian nationalism during the early period. The changes induced by foreign rule, it is here argued, were incomplete. This fact by itself suggests limitations upon the development of nationalism in India, limitations which make it misleading to equate that nationalism with the nationalisms created in western Europe as a concomitant of the industrial revolution and the wholesale transformation of European society. Moreover, these limitations help to account for the divergencies within emerging nationalism which form the subject of this study.

There was no single Indian response to Europeanization. Rather, there were many responses from different segments of the population. Some segments were considerably affected by European contact, other elements less so, and still others hardly at all. In addition, the Europeanization process was many-sided, and touched various parts of the indigenous population in different ways.[4] Thus, emerging nationalism in India had to consist of, or represent, a *variety* of reactions to the variegated experience with the West which was India's lot. In fact, one of the major problems facing the nationalist leadership was the need to *contain* so varied a set of responses within what had, for purposes of effective political action, to strive to become a unified movement.*

Even more basic was the need to create a widespread popular acceptance of the ideal of nationalism. To be effective, the nationalist leadership had to diffuse their doctrine as widely as possible in an environment which was largely unprepared for and in certain respects hostile to the idea of a single nation. The creation of Indian nationalism can be analyzed as a dynamic process, involving tension, action, and reaction between the minority of its proponents and the majority of Indians who were—because of

---

*Sri Aurobindo made this point quite effectively in an early, and largely overlooked, article he published on the Congress in the pages of the *Indu-Prakash* (Bombay), Aug. 21, 1893, under the title "New Lamps for Old." The article has been reprinted in easily accessible form in H. Mukherjee and U. Mukherjee, *Sri Aurobindo's Political Thought (1893-1908)* (Calcutta: F. Mukhopadhyay, 1958), p. 69-70. "In other words, the necessities of the political movement initiated by the Congress have brought into one place and for a common purpose all sorts and conditions of men, and so by smoothing away the harsher discrepancies between them has created a certain modicum of sympathy between classes that were more or less at variance."

their situation—apathetic, unprepared, or opposed. There were, at the same time, tension and conflict between the proponents of nationalism, sections of which advanced different goals, different strategies, and different justifications for nationalist activity.

There was also the problem that nationalism was but *one* of the possible responses by Indians to European contact and domination. There were, that is to say, aspects of Europeanization which did not create a basis for nationalism or which may—in their effects—have been antithetical to the growth of nationalism in India. European contact did not necessarily create nationalism. From this mélange of contrary impulses and effects arose the circumstances and conditions which shaped the course of growth of nationalism and which created those divergencies to which we refer.

But the matter of response to Europeanization is only part of the story. Equally important to the shaping of nationalism in the subcontinent was the fact that India did not comprise a homogeneous and well-knit population, or society—in other than rudimentary respects—prior to the coming of the Europeans. Lacking homogeneity and unity around a concept of statehood or national participation, traditional India was ill-equipped to face the complex process of Europeanization and its differential effects. That there were important unifying implications in foreign domination cannot be denied. That there were, at the same time, effects which did nothing to unify India can also not be denied. Nationalism reflected both tendencies, the unifying and the divergent. Understanding of the moving balance or fluctuation between the two, it is here argued, is necessary if a meaningful analysis is to be achieved.*

---

*It has, of course, been argued that an essential cultural and religious unity, a common and pervasive tradition, had been created in premodern India. One can select certain culture traits and values which were sufficiently diffused, both vertically and horizontally, through Indian society to give a kind of unity. I will argue, however, that many such instances are irrelevant —at least for the topic at hand—and that the salient fact of life in premodern India was its particularism and localism. Veneration of the cow may well have been one of those rudimentary traits which was common to Indians, but I have seen no convincing argument that it served to unite Indians in any manner which was meaningful for the creation of political unity in a modern nation.

Divergent developments within Indian nationalism may be indicated by citing some of the more obvious ways in which the process of Europeanization evoked varying responses among the Indian people. At the same time, attention can be focussed on the important divergencies in nationalist development which resulted.

To begin with, there was the simple fact of widely varying degrees of contact between Europeans and Indians. The British were never numerous in India, and they tended to cluster in the great port cities such as Bombay and Calcutta, and in a limited number of important inland towns. In such places, Indians, especially those who served the English in some capacity, came in rather frequent contact with the foreigner—whether for good or for ill—while in the vast and populous rural hinterland the appearance of a European was rare.[5] Similarly, Europeans and European artifacts tended to follow the major arteries of the new, interconnecting system of rails and surfaced roads. The people in the immediate vicinity of these alien instrumentalities were thereby thrown into contact with alien and potentially disturbing traits to a degree unknown by their more isolated countrymen.

As should be apparent, the effect of Europeanization on the indigenous economic system varied widely in degree as well as in kind. Some groups, such as native handicrafters, lost their hereditary occupations and their economic security as a result of the opening of the Indian market to European goods. Certain agriculturists, particularly those who happened to be favorably situated for the cultivation of select cash crops, benefitted materially from the European connection. Some peasants were relatively unaffected by the change to a market economy, while others clearly suffered deprivation and dislocation.[6] The responses of Indians to European rule varied with their experience in the new economic situation, as did their involvement in emerging nationalism.

Foreign education was a powerful factor in the growth of nationalism in India—probably as important as any other single factor—yet foreign education was spread most *unevenly* throughout India, especially in the period covered by this study.[7] While exact figures have not been collected for the period in question, it is clear that only a tiny minority of Indians, certainly no more than one percent, had secured Western higher education prior to 1905. More important, this minority was by no means a random sample of the Indian population. This lack of representativeness was especially marked among those who reached the upper levels of the English system of education established by the British in India. Certain regions, certain communities, certain castes, and certain economic classes had much greater access to Western education or were more willing to pursue Western training. This was true either because location gave them greater access to European centers and to Western educational institutions, or because by historical accident the Europeans were settled for a longer time in their area. Again, it may have been because their community or caste was traditionally more inclined to look upon literacy favorably or had a tradition of literate occupation.* Finally, it may have been because their family was financially better equipped to bear the costs of Western education.

If Western education was the basis for nationalism in India, it is also clear that the various segments of the Indian population had substantially different degrees of access to that education, while certain classes or communities had greater motivation to acquire Western training. The 19th-century renaissance in Bengal, which was not to be duplicated in kind or in intensity elsewhere in India prior to the 20th century, stands as striking testimony to the exceptional experience with Europeans and with Western education which befell the Bengalis as contrasted with other Indians.† Moreover, vocal nationalism, on Western lines, appeared in Bengal sooner than in other parts of India. Bengal clearly had a majority of all Western-educated Indians during

*Certain groups were, for instance, early thrown in close contact with Europeans as their agents, or associates in trade. A knowledge of the English language and of English mercantile and bookkeeping methods would stand these persons or families in good stead, and their sons would be more likely to undertake Western training than would the sons of families not so situated.

†For a discussion of the socio-religious origins of the intellectual renaissance which stirred Bengal and which inspired a new group of spokesmen and authors, see the accounts to be found in A. Rajam, *The National Congress, Its Evolution* (Madras: Sons of India, 1918), pp. 9-16. Also, H. Mukherjee and U. Mukherjee, *The Growth of Nationalism in India* (Calcutta: Presidency Library, 1957), pp. 39-41, 51-57.

the early period as well as a preponderance of the existing institutions of higher education.

It should, however, be noted that Western education had a dual effect. On the one hand, it served as an important unifying agent for those who were its graduates. At the same time, it sharply distinguished the minority group of graduates from the rest of society. That is to say, Indians who received a Western education shared a common and unifying intellectual experience, but a vast gulf was created between the college graduate and the masses. As Professor Aggarwala has put it in commenting on the educated leaders of the early Congress Party:

> But in the beginning it [the Congress] was not a movement of the masses. It represented and claimed to speak only for the intelligentsia of the Indian society. It was not even a middle class movement. With the exception of Lokmanya Tilak and possibly a few others, most of its leaders were out of touch with the masses.[8]

This, of course, created a major difficulty for the nationalist leadership in its attempt to secure a popular following. The Westernized intelligentsia was imbued with values and goals derived from English education which were virtually unintelligible, at least at certain critical points, to the masses they sought to lead. Western training turned the attention of its devotees to Western ideals and institutions which were alien to Indian experience. Two recent authors have pointed this up in discussing the role of Aurobindo Ghose in the development of Indian nationalism and his opposition to the early Congress leadership:

> He [Aurobindo] felt the utter unsoundness of recognizing England as the sole exemplar of India's political progress. He found the Congress politics rooted in shallow earth, divorced from the historic traditions of the country. He felt the need of introducing new blood into the body of the Congress and revitalizing it by calling the masses into it. . . . At Baroda he felt his breach with the Congress widening with the degree of his Indianisation growing as its natural consequence. He found the Congress too much Occidental in outlook and temper, fixed in its narrow ideals. . . .[9]

In short, the intelligentsia tended to petition Parliament for redress of grievances such as the lack of Indian representation in the Legislative Councils. This was hardly a topic calculated to arouse an illiterate peasantry who had never heard of parliaments, legislatures, or electoral colleges.

But there is more to the story than the effect of Western education in separating the new elite from the tradition-bound masses. Western education did not affect all recipients in the same way, even though it represented a common intellectual experience. It is incorrect to think of a *single* response to the alien values and methods inculcated by the English system of education. While much more research needs to be done on Indian responses to Western training, it is possible to discern at least two major variants among the responses of the Western-educated. Each of these types of response was to bear fruit in its effect upon the kind of nationalism espoused by the persons involved.

Of these the first may be called the "modernist" or "reformist" response, while the second can be described as "traditionalist" or "revivalist." Neither of these polar response-types can be overlooked if we are to understand the contrary trends implicit in the evolution of Indian nationalism. Both of these responses, so contradictory in their assumptions, values, and objectives, can be identified quite clearly among those who received Western education and among the nationalist leaders.*

The modernist or reformist response was dominant among the founders of the Indian Association and of the better-known Congress Party and has remained a major element of these associations down to the present day. In the period under discussion, the representatives of the reformist viewpoint comprised the Moderate group within the Congress and set the tone for the Congress movement. The Moderates valued the British connection with India and wanted to preserve that connection. They were as interested in social reform, along Western lines, as in political ad-

---

*Unfortunately, to complicate matters, one can make no neat and consistent dichotomy between reformers and revivalists. Some leaders seemed to combine features of both positions in themselves, so as to hold one position on certain matters and the other position on other matters. Also, some leaders changed camps during their careers. Some began and earned fame as traditionalists only to become modernists later in life. It is my view that this reflects the complexity of the mixture of Western and indigenous values in recent India. Presumably, for purposes of analysis, the most fruitful procedure will be to place the representatives of the various viewpoints along a continuum, to locate and demark clusters of views along the continuum, and to use the information as the basis for creation of a typology.

vancement and sought a voice in government so as to be able to facilitate the renovation and modernization of India. Of them, Sir Henry Cotton, a senior official in the Indian Civil Service, once said:

> They are loyal in that they appreciate the advantages of British rule, and are grateful to the British government for the benefits which have been conferred upon them. . . . But they are embittered, deeply embittered, at their exclusion from power. . . . They claim that the Government should repose confidence in them, and not shrink from raising them to the highest posts in civil and military life. They demand real, not nominal, equality, a voice in the government of their own country, and a career in the public service.[10]

The Hindu traditionalist or revivalist response to Western values also became a prominent factor in nationalist circles during the period prior to 1905 and has remained a part of the political scene since that time. The revivalists who entered the Congress clustered in the so-called Extremist wing of that organization and sought to wrest control of the Congress from the Moderates.

The revivalists reacted against Western education as a perceived threat to their values, their social system, and their ancient religion. The revivalist response was given its first systematic statement by Swami Dayanand Saraswati, who founded the Arya Samaj as a militant defense organization for Hinduism.[11] His movement was based upon a return to the *Vedas* and a denunciation of Western-style reforms.

> Swami Dayanand, however, based it [the Arya Samaj] on the bedrock of the Vedas. It was Hinduism pure and aggressive. Naturally, therefore, it fostered more pride in the country, and the feeling it fostered of the purity and greatness of Hinduism was bound to have an encouraging and elevating effect on a people weighed down with a consciousness of their own inferiority.[12]

It was, however, Bal Tilak, the Poona Brahmin, who made revivalist nationalism a powerful force within Indian nationalism. Tilak, leader of the Extremists, was the fiery editor of two prominent nationalist newspapers. Through these organs, Tilak pressed his nationalist and revivalist propaganda and developed his ideas for quickening national self-consciousness by use of religious themes. Tilak was one of the first to make genuine efforts to spread nationalism as a doctrine among the uneducated villagers and residents of the small *mofussil* towns. In 1893 he launched the popular Hindu Ganpati Festival and, shortly thereafter, the Shivaji Festival. In these festivals, Hindu students and other youth learned the secret of organized action in defense of their Motherland.[13]

Thus there were at least two major variants of response to Western training, which were reflected in major and contradictory movements within developing nationalism. The two were diametrically opposite, for the first embraced Western science and logic, modernization and secular democracy, while the second turned back to Hinduism, or to the sacred books such as the *Vedas*, for justification of the Indian way of life against the challenge of the West.[14] Within the nationalist movement the result was the creation of rival organizations and bitter contest over the direction to be taken by nationalism and by the Congress.

The kinds of divergencies already mentioned by no means exhaust the list. Understanding the growth of nationalism in the subcontinent requires analysis of the role of other divergent or conflicting impulses, each of which had somehow to be contained within nationalism if the carefully built edifice was not to be torn asunder. Study of these contrary impulses sharpens our insight and helps to explain what may loosely be called the "dialectic" of nationalist development.

Perhaps the most obvious and best known instance of widely divergent development in the course of evolution of nationalism in the subcontinent was the rise of a clearly separatist Muslim nationalism which led to the subsequent partitioning of the subcontinent between India and Pakistan. The rise of Muslim nationalism in India and its complete separation from what may be called the main stream of Nationalist evolution among the non-Muslims is, however, a special case and merits full-scale study in its own right. In this essay it is not possible to include more than a very few comments on Muslim separatism.[15]

Muslim separatism in India reflected several of the divergencies inherent in the modern Indian scene. There was, for instance, difference between the religious, social, and cultural tradition of Islam and that of Hinduism. In addition, the Muslims as a community clearly had less access to—and probably less motivation for—Western education than the communities of Hindus. The difference between the percent of Muslims who had received high Western education prior to 1905 and the percent of Hindus with similar training is very striking, with a much larger proportion of Hindus being among the Western-trained. This meant, *inter alia,* a serious difference, at least from the point of view of the Muslims, in Muslim access to government employment at any level. It also put the Muslims at a disadvantage in the contest for elected office when representative institutions began to be established in the subcontinent. It is noteworthy that the Muslim League first coalesced around the issue of separate representation for Muslims in legislative councils.

By and large, the Muslim areas of India were more isolated from large-scale European habitation than were the predominantly Hindu areas. The Northwest Frontier region, a Muslim heartland, was among the last regions of India to come under effective British administration and substantial British contact. Unlike many groups among the Hindus, few Muslims were members of commercial or clerical groupings which soon found reason for sustained contact with the British. Among the Muslim leaders, a substantial element were rural landlords who had comparatively little reason to pursue Western knowledge or to become involved in Western patterns of behavior. On a number of scores, then, the Muslims lagged behind the Hindus in their exposure to Western ways and in their acceptance of the new system of power and of education. By the end of the 19th century, Muslim leadership had become acutely aware of the ensuing disadvantages, and the tendency toward a separate Muslim nationalism became pronounced. British policy, in certain respects, favored this result. The central point, however, is that situational factors underlay this prominent divergence within emerging nationalism.

Nationalism in India has usually been viewed as an all-India phenomenon, and it is correct to say that it played an all-India role and frequently had all-India goals. Nonetheless, a consistent and significant aspect of nationalism has been the conflict or dissonance between a deep-seated regionalism and parochialism on the one hand and Indian nationalism on the other. This regional ism, in part, reflected the previously noted fact that Western con tact was more persistent and effective in some areas than in others. But it also reflected prominent characteristics of traditional Indian society which emphasized local group and community cohesion. In addition, regionalism of a socio-cultural and economic character—so typical of a traditional society—was reinforced by the existence of separate, major languages which were regionally based.* Prior to the 20th century, regionalism was given added potency by the virtual absence of an adequate system of transportation and communications on an all-India basis. Movement out of one's own locality was difficult and expensive.

In the late 19th century, regionalism was one of the most distinctive characteristics of the growing nationalism. In those years it was probably more accurate to speak of Bengali nationalism, of Maharashtrian nationalism, or of Punjabi nationalism, than to speak of Indian nationalism. Without understanding the role of Bengali nationalism or of Punjabi nationalism, as well as the intricate links which developed around certain issues *between* the two, we shall not understand the complex process which brought Indian nationalism into being. Some work has been done on the basis of provincial nationalism in India, but very little has been done to analyze the emergence of interconnections between provincial forces. The latter created a delicately balanced all-India nationalism and structured it in certain ways.

Another divergence in the growth of nationalism has been between the interests, objectives, and attitudes of the urban sector of Indian society and those of the rural sector. Nationalism meant certain things to the people in the cities—where the literacy rate was higher and where the Western factory system and business enterprise were concentrated—and rather different things to the masses who lived, as had their forefathers, in the traditionalist,

---

*In quite recent years the Government of India has had to face the fact of regional and linguistic provincialism which has, on occasion, erupted into violence. Bombay has, for example, witnessed strife between speakers of Marathi and of Gujarati. On this topic, see Selig Harrison, *The Most Dangerous Decades* (Princeton: Princeton University Press, 1960). Also, Joan Bondurant, *Regionalism versus Provincialism: A Study in Problems of Indian National Unity* (Berkeley: University of California, 1958, Indian Press Digests-Monograph Series, No. 4).

agrarian villages.[16] This would have been the case, if for no other reason, because it was in the cities that the nascent middle class congregated. Moreover, almost all of the nationalist newspapers were published in the cities, and their readership was predominantly urban. Town residents became aware of European political ideas and instrumentalities sooner and more directly than did millions in rural areas.*

Urban interests in support of nationalism were different from those of the rural population. The mercantile and early industrial magnates of India supported nationalism because of the conflict, real or potential, between their enterprise and that of the British. This was essentially an urban phenomenon, while the class which wanted government employment was largely urban rather than rural. The ease and practicability of organization and of combination was much greater in the cities and towns than in the half million villages. For years the bulk of the resolutions passed by the annual Congress sessions were concerned with issues which were primarily of interest to the city-dwellers, while most of the delegates to the various Congress sessions were from towns. In addition, the rural-based landlords tended to develop their own political associations and to shy away from the Congress.

In the period up to the Partition of Bengal, this dichotomy posed a major problem for the growth of nationalism. The nationalist message was confined largely to the towns. But if there was to be an Indian nationalism, the rural majority had to be involved. The nationalist leadership of that period was, by and large, incapable of appealing to the villagers in terms that would rouse them. The search for an effective appeal to the village was to have a profound effect at a later date.

This paper is not designed to extend the list of divergent developments, but rather to indicate their nature and their significance for an adequate understanding of nationalism as a

---

*After World War I, Mahatma Gandhi "revolutionized" Indian nationalism by carrying it for the first time in any effective fashion to the villages. Tilak had made efforts in this direction in Maharashtria before Gandhi, and Sri Aurobindo had dwelt upon the importance of such a development, but Tilak's attempt was premature and he failed to develop a consistent and effective rural appeal on other than a local basis.

complex development. Its aim is to lay the basis for analysis of the effects of social change upon the kinds of nationalism which emerged. In this connection it envisages creation of a typology for the variety of nationalisms which arose in modern India.

Nationalism has been described as a general phenomenon attributable to Indians, but such a view is neither useful nor tenable. That view robs scholarship of significant vantage points from which to pose crucial questions regarding the interplay of factors in the emergence of nationalism. At the same time it leaves unexamined certain fragilities which continue to be important in Indian nationalism in the more recent period.

NOTES

1. Reference is made to such standard titles as: B. Pattabhi Sitaramayya, *The History of the Indian National Congress* (2 vols.; Bombay: Padma Publications, 1946); V. P. Raghuvanshi, *Indian Nationalist Movement and Thought* (Agra: L. Agarwal, 1951); C. Y. Chintamani, *Indian Politics since the Mutiny* (London: Allen & Unwin, 1940); R. C. Majumdar, H. C. Raychaudhuri, and K. Datta, *An Advanced History of India* (2nd ed.; London: Macmillan, 1950).
2. An effort to study the development of Indian nationalism in terms of "stages of growth" has been made by R. I. Crane, "The Leadership of the Congress Party," in R. L. Park and I. Tinker (eds.), *Leadership and Political Institutions in India* (Princeton: Princeton University Press, 1959), pp. 169-187.
3. *Ibid.*, p. 169.
4. I have discussed this matter in two previous articles: "India: A Study of the Impact of Western Civilization," *Social Education*, XV (1951), 365-371; "Strata Disruption and Social Change in South Asia," *United Asia*, VI (1954), 228-234. See also the discussions in K. Chattopadhyay (ed.), *Study of Changes in Traditional Culture* (Calcutta: University of Calcutta, 1957).
5. Bernard Cohn has recently demonstrated the process by which certain Indians were thrown in close juxtaposition with the Europeans and/or served as agents to the Europeans. In his view a new class was thus created which, at the least, had a special interest in the maintenance of the British connection. See his article: "The Initial British Impact on India: A Case Study of the Benares Region," *Journal of Asian Studies*, XIX (1950), 418-431. The article stresses the fact that members of this group opposed the nationalist objectives of the English-educated and urbanized Indians.
6. The uneven and varied effect of English rule on Indian agrarian society is well documented in T. F. Shea, "The Land System of Malabar and Its Influence upon Capital Formation in Agriculture" (unpublished dissertation, University of Pennsylvania, 1959).
7. B. T. McCully, *English Education and the Origins of Indian Nationalism* (New York: Columbia University Press, 1940), presents an invaluable account of the spread of Western education in India and its effects. Also,

R. N. Aggarwala, *National Movement and Constitutional Development of India* (Delhi: Metropolitan Book Co., 1956), p. 35: ". . . none can deny that the first demand for self-governing institutions in India came from those who had acquired the western education."

8. R. N. Aggarwala, *op. cit.*, p. 42. Also, M. A. Buch, *Rise and Growth of Indian Militant Nationalism* (Baroda: Atmaram Press, 1940), p. 6-7: "The [early] Congress movement was not a popular movement. The leaders did not care to enlist popular enthusiasm or interest. The movement was therefore confined deliberately to the intelligentsia only."

9. H. Mukherjee and U. Mukherjee, *Sri Aurobindo's Political Thought (1893-1908)* (Calcutta: F. Mukhopadhyay, 1958), p. 22. Also M. Buch, *op. cit.*, p. 43: "Mass movements require mass leaders, and the Congress politicians, with a few exceptions, had so far specialized in the leadership of academic audiences. Tilak [by contrast] had been working with the people, addressing his appeal to them in a language which they could understand. . . ."

10. Sir Henry Cotton, *New India: or, India in Transition* (London: Kegan Paul, Trench, Trubner, 1907), pp. 40-41.

11. For the life of Swami Dayanand see the biography by Har B. Sarda, *Life of Dayanand Saraswati* (Ajmere: Vedic Yantiakaya, 1946).

12. A. Rajam, *op. cit.*, p. 5.

13. Several volumes have been published recently on Tilak. See D. V. Tahmankar, *Lokamanya Tilak, Father of Indian Unrest* (London: John Murray, 1956). Also, M. Buch, *op. cit.*, p. 125, speaking of the religious festivals organized by Tilak, says, "Tilak was thus able to effect the union of the new political spirit with the tradition and sentiment of the historic past and of both with the ineradicable religious temperament of the people, of which these festivals were the symbol."

14. Another division in the ranks of nationalism was represented by the formation and long-time existence of the Indian Association, founded in Calcutta in 1876. Though the Indian Association at times worked rather closely with the Congress, it generally preferred its own course of action. For a useful historical account, see J. C. Bagal, *History of the Indian Association, 1876-1951* (Calcutta: H. N. Mazumdar, 1953).

15. The material in print on Muslim nationalism is rather limited and is generally less adequate than the material on the Congress or on "Hindu" nationalism. No substantial study of Muslim nationalism has as yet been published. However, for general insights, see: Sir H. V. Lovett, *A History of the Indian Nationalist Movement* (New York: F. A. Stokes, 1920); W. R. Smith, *Nationalism and Reform in India* (New Haven: Yale University Press, 1938); W. C. Smith, *The Muslim League, 1942-45* (Lahore: Minerva Book Shop, 1945), as well as his major volume, *Modern Islam in India* (Lahore: Ripon Press, 1947).

16. I have discussed the scope of urbanism in India and some of the significant differences between the Indian urban and rural milieus in "Urbanism in India," *American Journal of Sociology*, LX (1955), 463-470. Sir Henry Cotton, *op. cit.*, has also remarked on the gap between the urban and rural milieu in India.

Hindu Concepts and the Gita in Early Indian National Thought

MINOO ADENWALLA

Lawrence College

This paper is a study of the use of religious concepts and literature in moving a tradition-directed, politically unconscious, agrarian society to political action, and in inculcating among a mass whose value structure directed their identification toward the joint family, the caste, the community, and the village a feeling of nationalism and patriotism toward the nation state. Other segments of Indian society were also expected to respond to this call of nationalism interpreted through the language of religion: the university student exposed to a new cultural impact, who assimilated modern values imperfectly and therefore reacted against them; the industrial worker, rootless and insecure within the complexity of a technological system he did not understand; and some highly placed orthodox caste groups who saw in the growing secularization of Indian society the destruction of their own firmly held religio-cultural beliefs and a threat to their own positions of power and status.

History knows the political elite that led this movement as the Extremists, in contrast to those called the Moderates who controlled the Indian National Congress from its founding in 1885 to 1915. The Moderates represented the new professional Westernized middle class whose outlook was conditioned by the recently inaugurated Western educational system. They sought to transplant within India the social and political philosophies of nineteenth-century England. They valued British rule for having brought India order and security, and for having evolved methods of reform that would preserve this peace: constitutional agitation from the political platform; the training of Indian leaders in the techniques of parliamentary democracy through making the Congress act as the "loyal opposition" to this rule; and the use of educated public opinion to further a doctrine of social reform. The Moderates also expected the British government itself to create, slowly but surely, the beginnings of democratic institutions and to associate the representatives of "enlightened" Indian thought with them. The Moderates shunned mass participation in the movement, for they believed such action would jeopardize their opportunity of creating an India democratic not only in the realm of politics, but in that of social relations also.

The immediate aim of the Extremists, in contrast, was the expulsion of both Western power and influence from India. Their leaders postulated the superiority of Hindu religion and culture over all others; they attempted to revive what they considered to be the active, ancient spirit of a "golden age" of Hinduism, a spirit which would free the country from its bondage to and imitation of England and the West.

Our aim here is to examine how two of the most respected and influential of this elite—Bal Gangadhar Tilak and Aravindo Ghose—utilized the Hindu concepts of karma and dharma, and the *Bhagavat Gita* to transmit a message of nationalism and political action.

Tilak led the Hindu revival in politics in Maharashtra, Ghose in Bengal. Under their leadership the Indian national movement witnessed for the first time mass political action in the form of strikes, demonstrations, processions, and economic boycott, political action that culminated in the *Swadeshi* movement following Lord Curzon's partition of the province of Bengal, in 1905.

> The twin movement of Boycott and Swadeshi constitutes an important landmark in the development of national consciousness. It was the forerunner of the subsequent Non-co-operation movements launched under the leadership of Mahatma Gandhi. It gave the national movement a truly popular character by providing it with sound foundation in the active support of the masses.[1]

Through their writings and speeches, Tilak and Ghose hoped to arouse village and working-class India; not the India of the already Westernized professional classes which already dominated the Indian National Congress, but the industrial workers of the mills, the masses who toiled in the fields, the young school boy and university student. As Ghose wrote:

> The proletariat is as I have striven to show the real key of the situation. Torpid he is and immobile; he is nothing of an actual force, but he is a very great potential force, and whoever succeeds in understanding and elicting his strength becomes by the very fact master of the future.[2]

To arouse this proletariat made up often of men who could not read or write, of those to whom the very language of any form of Western political thought was meaningless, it was necessary to speak in understandable terms. Few terms were more familiar to the Hindu masses than *karma,* the law of fate that resulted through one's own actions, and *dharma,* one's religious duty in life.

Tilak and Ghose popularized the concept of nationalism as being the new dharma or religious duty of India. Preaching a doctrine of religion being nationalism, Ghose wrote:

> Nationalism is not a mere political programme; Nationalism is a religion that has come from God; Nationalism is a creed which you shall have to love. If you are going to be a Nationalist, if you are going to assent to this religion of Nationalism, you must do it in the religious spirit. You must remember that you are the instruments of God.[3]

Through nationalism would come spiritual transformation; but it would take men of daring and sacrifice like the Hindu *Kshatriyas* to accompish this task:

> The New Nationalism is an attempt at a spiritual transformation of the nineteenth century Indian; it is a notice of dismissal or at least of suspension to the bourgeois and all his ideas and ways and works. It is a call for the men of faith . . . the prophets, martyrs, the kshatriyas, the samurai, the initiators of revolution.[4]

Nationalism was the new dharma because India herself was something divine and mystic; she was the great Mother (*Bharat Mata*), much more than mere earth and stone and people:

> It is not till the Motherland reveals herself to the eye of the mind as something more than a stretch of earth or a mass of individuals, it is not till she takes shape as a great Divine and Maternal Power in a form of beauty that can dominate the

mind and seize the heart that these petty fears and hopes vanish in the all-absorbing passion for the Mother and her service, and the patriotism that works miracles and saves a doomed nation is born.[5]

Tilak also taught that the karma of those who worked in observance of this law of national dharma would be the aid of God himself. Action performed was destined to bear its just fruit, even though the performer himself might not be present to witness the result of a free, independent India:

The effect of action (*karma*) cannot fail to take its place in this world. The effect of this action may not be obtained so soon as I say, may not be obtained before my eyes. But this action must have its fruit . . . According to the law of action, when a certain action is done, another results from it, and a third one results out of that. Such succession goes on . . . Make the effort that is to be made. Be ready to do this work with the thought that it belongs to you. I am sure that by the grace of God your next generation will not fail to obtain the fruit of this work, though it may not be obtained in your lifetime.[6]

Tilak also appealed to the *Rigveda* to justify this call to action:

If perils overtake us we are prepared to bear them. They must be borne . . . Then God will not abandon you: such is my conviction. These things will be achieved by the grace of God. But we must work. There is a very old principle that God helps them who help themselves. The principle occurs in the *Rigveda*. God becomes incarnate.[7]

However, no one single piece of scripture was of greater aid to Tilak and Ghose in transmitting their message of political activism than the text of the *Bhagavat Gita*. For though Hinduism has no central canon such as the Bible or the Koran, the *Gita* has come to be looked upon "as the most authoritative expression of Hindu thought."[8] Nikhilananda in his translation of the *Upanishads* comments, "Sri Krishna, in his dialogue with Arjuna, presented through the *Bhagavat Gita* the essence of the *Upanishads*." [9]

It appears in the great epic of Hinduism, the *Mahabharata*. However, the *Gita* itself is considered an addition to the actual text. Most commentators are generally agreed that by the sixth century A.D. the *Mahabharata* was known throughout India. Through the services of Brahmin storytellers who wandered through the land, even the poorest farmer in his isolated village came to hear of the epic war between the Pandavas and the Kurus. The *Gita*'s setting is the battlefield of Kurukshetra. Arjuna, the hero of the Pandavas, is despondent, for on the morrow he will war against the Kurus, who are not only enemies but also his kinsmen. The *Bhagavat Gita* (the Lord's Song) itself is in the form of a dialogue between Arjuna and Lord Krishna, who appears before him to tell him what man's duty in this world is. As K. M. Panikkar writes:

> The *Gita* is primarily religious in its teaching. Its context is man's dejection in the face of duty which seems to him not only unpleasant but wholly abhorrent to his being. Its surrounding is a battlefield on which two mighty armies are arrayed; but the person who asks for advice is the first man of the age, *nara* the representative human being, and the Preceptor speaks with the voice of supreme authority, of God.[10]

Krishna urges Arjuna to perform his duty or dharma through battle, even if it means death for the Kurus; for they have already been slain by God, and he, Arjuna, is no more than an instrument of the Divine. Krishna also expounds, during the course of the dialogue, on the three great paths to union with God: the path of *Bhakti* or devotion; the path of *Gnana* Yoga or knowledge; and the path of karma Yoga or the path of right action without expectation of reward or result. Traditional commentaries on the *Gita,* like that of the eighth-century sage Sankaracharya, supported a theory of renunciation: man, upon achievement of union with God, gave up the world and lived in the life of the spirit. The path of action, therefore, was secondary and of lesser importance.

This paper is not really concerned with the question of *the* correct religious interpretation of the *Gita.* However, it seems fairly clear that taken literally and in a historical sense, it can be made to justify violence and war, if such is done through a feeling of righteousness, through action uncommitted to its fruits or rewards. Later in the national movement Gandhi used the *Gita* in support of his theory of nonviolence, holding that the work had to be taken symbolically, that the battlefield of Kurukshetra was in reality man's soul. But to Ghose and Tilak, who both wrote long and learned commentaries on the *Gita*, the sacred text justified the use of violence in a righteous cause. As Tilak said: "We may kill even our teachers and our kinsmen and no blame attaches if we are not actuated by selfish motives."[11] And Aravindo Ghose in his commentary on the *Gita* wrote:

> War and destruction are not only a universal principle of our life here in its purely material aspects, but also of our mental and moral existence . . . It is impossible, at least as men and things are, to advance, to grow, to fulfil and still to observe really and utterly that principle of harmlessness which is yet placed before us as the highest and best law of conduct . . . Even soul-force, when it is effective, destroys . . . Therefore the command of God (Krishna) to the Aryan: 'Destroy when by destruction the world must advance, but hate not that which thou destroyest.' [12]

Tilak actually held that his was the definitive interpretation of the *Gita*, for his study was motivated solely in discovering the real truth, and in vindicating no preconceived theory:

> Various commentators have put as many interpretations on the book, and surely the writer or composer could not have written or composed the book for so many interpretations being put on it. He must have but one meaning and one purpose running through the book, and that I have tried to find out. I believe I have succeeded in it, because having no theory of mine for which I sought any support from the book so universally respected, I had no reason to twist the text to suit my theory.[13]

He then goes on to state the conclusion at which his study arrived:

> The conclusion I have come to is that the *Gita* advocates the performance of action in this world even after the actor has achieved the highest union with the Supreme Deity by *Gnana* (knowledge) or *Bhakti* (Devotion). This action must be done to keep the world going by the right path of evolution which the Creator has destined the world to follow. In order that the action may not bind the actor it must be done with the aim of helping his purpose and without any attachment to the coming result. This I hold is the lesson of the *Gita*.[14]

Tilak does not deny the path of gnana Yoga or bhakti Yoga. For him, however, both are subservient to the path of activism and action—the path of karma Yoga. Further justifying this conclusion, he refers to the *Gita's* historical context. Unlike Gandhi, he does not choose to treat Kurukshetra as the battlefield of the soul:

> If the *Gita* was preached to desponding Arjuna to make him ready for the fight—for the action—how can it be said that the ultimate lesson of the great book is *Bhakti* or *Gnana* alone.[15]

Following almost the very same line of argument, Aravindo Ghose, in his *Essays on the Gita*, wrote:

> There are those who make the *Gita* teach not works at all, but a discipline of preparation for renouncing life and works. . . . It is quite easy to justify this view by citations from the book and by certain arrangement of stress in following out its argument. . . . But it is quite impossible to persist in this view on an impartial reading in face of the continual assertion to the very end that action should be preferred to inaction and that superiority lies with the true, the inner renunciation of desire by the giving up of works to the supreme Purusha.[16]

Action in this world was important since union with God without a concern for the good of one's neighbour was imperfect. The world itself was created by the Universal Will; and on becoming part of that very Will, Man could not disregard this creation; it was part of the divinely ordained plan that he continue to serve it:

> Man strives to gain union with God; and when this union is achieved the individual Will merges with the mighty Universal Will. When this is achieved will the individual say: "I shall do no action, and I shall not help the world."—the world which is because the Will with which he has sought union has willed it to be so? . . . If man seeks unity with the Deity, he must necessarily seek unity with the interests of the world also, and work for it. If he does not, then the unity is not perfect, because there is union between two elements out of the 3 (man and Deity), and the third (the world) is left out.[17]

Had Tilak and Ghose interpreted the *Gita* traditionally, had they held that once Man achieved union (*Moksha*) he renounced the world, since he now realized that it was nothing more than *Maya* or illusion, it would have been impossible for them to have used the text as a call to political action. But if action dedicated to God was the message of the *Gita,* if the text could be interpreted in a historical context so as to sanction war and violence, and if the new dharma demanded service and sacrifice for Mother India, then all action directed against the new Kurus— the British government of India—was justifiable, no matter what form it took. And the age-old law of karma assured final victory in this just cause, for the seed of such action, once planted, was cosmically ordained to bear fruit.

Indian history gives no true example of large-scale political action on the part of the mass of the people. For politics and government were the tasks of the ruler and his chosen advisors. Village India lived its own life. Men like Tilak and Ghose succeeded in giving these very people a form of political consciousness, a desire for independence, a feeling of patriotism and nationalism, a motivation to participate in the liberation of their country. They showed for the first time how it was possible to arouse a poor, tradition-bound, politically unconscious mass of people to political action through the use of cultural techniques of appeal that were understandable to them.

NOTES

1. K. R. Bombwall, *Indian Politics since 1885* (Delhi: Atam Ram, 1951), p. 85.
2. Aravindo Ghose, as quoted in S. Mitra, *The Liberator* (Bombay: Jaico Publishing House, 1954), p. 38.
3. *Ibid.,* p. 101.
4. *Ibid.,* pp. 122-123.
5. *Ibid.,* p. 70.
6. B. G. Tilak, *His Writings and Speeches* (3rd ed., Madras: Ganesh and Co., 1922), p. 192.
7. *Ibid.,* p. 199.
8. K. M. Panikkar, *The Indian Revolution* (Bombay: National Information and Publications, 1951), p. 17.
9. Swami Nikhilananda, *The Upanishads* (New York: Harper, 1908), pp. 10-11.
10. K. M. Panikkar, *The Indian Revolution,* pp. 17-18.
11. B. G. Tilak, as quoted in K. R. Bombwall, *Indian Politics since 1885,* p. 82.
12. Aravindo Ghose, as quoted in S. Mitra, *The Liberator,* p. 124.
13. B. G. Tilak, *His Writings and Speeches,* p. 232.
14. *Ibid.,* p. 233.
15. *Ibid.,* p. 234.
16. Aravindo Ghose, *Essays on the Gita* (Calcutta: Arya Publishing House, 1926), p. 41.
17. B. G. Tilak, *His Writings and Speeches,* pp. 234-235.

Allocation of Investment in India

PHILIP S. THOMAS

Grinnell College

The problem of investment criteria in underdeveloped areas has been the subject of great attention during the past decade. The basic question is this: Given the limited quantity of saving or investment funds available, how should these funds be allocated? Economists have given increasingly complex answers to this question, with the range of suggested criteria including the capital-labor ratio,[1] the capital-output ratio,[2] the social marginal product,[3] the marginal per capita reinvestment quotient,[4] and the marginal growth contribution.[5] Among these, the criterion which continues to enjoy the greatest prestige among noneconomists, and many economists as well, is the capital-labor ratio. It is part of the "conventional wisdom" (to borrow J. K. Galbraith's phrase[6]) that labor-intensive investments are the most efficient, particularly for overpopulated, underdeveloped countries.

It is the purpose of this paper to point out the weaknesses of the labor-intensive criterion, to present certain alternative criteria, and to show how the latter better explain the investment allocation in India—an overpopulated country par excellence. Before proceeding with this critique, however, it is essential to present the case for labor-intensity.

It is tempting to believe that the allocation of investment is a relatively simple matter, at least at the theoretical level: projects should be selected which will result in a maximum rate of economic growth. But what does this mean?

First: Is the goal to maximize national income or per capita income? If the latter, the population impact of an investment, as well as its impact on output, must be considered.

24

Second: Is the goal to maximize output in the immediate future, or is it the ultimate level of output (or its rate of growth) in the distant future which is our concern? In the former case, short-lived, high-output investments might be best; in the latter case, the most durable capital equipment might be most suitable.

Third: Is the achievement and maintenance of full employment a proper goal of economic growth? If output is our sole concern, then modern, labor-saving devices might be the most desirable methods in which to invest. But if unemployment accentuates the economic injustice of income inequality and leads to social and political instability, then all economic growth might cease. In this case, the employment aspects of investment assume major importance.

The phrasing of these three questions suggests that the alternative goals are necessarily in conflict: the satisfaction of one, maximizing output, for example, seems to preclude the satisfaction of another, such as full employment. This need not be the case, however, as the labor-intensive hypothesis holds out the possibility that all of these goals might be attained simultaneously.

The labor-intensive hypothesis may be stated as follows:* In countries where labor is plentiful and cheap, and capital is scarce and expensive, the most efficient method of production, i.e., that one which will maximize output from the given resources available, will be relatively labor-intensive. The figures in Table I will

TABLE I.

| COUNTRY A: | CAPITAL STOCK: | $10 | |
	POPULATION (LABOR FORCE)	10 MEN	
		Technique 1 Capital-intensive	Technique 2 Labor-intensive
1. Capital-labor ratio		$10/1	$10/10 or $1/1
2. Total output		$5.00	$10.00
3. Output per capita		$ .50	$ 1.00
4. Output per worker employed		$5.00	$ 1.00

*In this initial presentation of the labor-intensive criterion, the case for it will be made as clear and strong as possible. The weaknesses of the criterion will be discussed in later sections of the paper.

be used to illustrate this point. Country A has a capital stock of ten dollars, and a population and labor force of ten men. It is assumed that two of the alternative techniques available to Country A are Technique 1, which is capital-intensive (the capital-labor ratio is $10/1), and Technique 2, which is labor-intensive (the capital-labor ratio is $10/10, or $1/1). It is further assumed that if the entire capital stock is employed in Technique 1, the total output will be five dollars, and if the capital stock is employed in Technique 2, the total output will be ten dollars. This relationship between the outputs of the two techniques is based on the economic principle of diminishing returns or variable proportions. That is, as additional units of labor are employed with a given amount of capital, total output increases, but at a diminishing rate. Thus, when ten men are employed with the capital stock, the capital is being used more intensively so that greater output results than when one man is employed, but the increase in output is not tenfold. Given the population, per capita output (income) will be the highest when the total output is greatest, as shown in Line 3 of Table I. With Technique 2, per capita income is one dollar, whereas with Technique 1, it is only fifty cents.

An unfortunate confusion has arisen between maximizing output *per capita* and output per *worker employed*. It is sometimes argued that since improving the productivity of the labor force, by having better methods and more capital for laborers to work with, is at the heart of economic growth, the best technique to employ is that one which maximizes the output of the individual worker employed.[7] That this is not the case is clearly shown in Table I. Technique 1 combines ten dollars capital with only one worker, so that his output is high, five dollars (Line 4). The output of the rest of the labor force, however, is zero because they are unemployed. When the ten dollars capital is combined with ten workers, the output per worker is only one dollar (because each worker has less capital to work with), but the total output is ten dollars, and thus per capita output (income) is higher.

On the basis of the principle of diminishing returns, therefore, relatively labor-intensive methods of production will yield the maximum output in the overpopulated, capital-scarce countries.

What will be the impact of labor-intensive investments on population growth? No clear-cut answer can be given, but a plausible argument can be made along the following lines. Since increasing the death rate as a method of population control does not seem to command widespread support,[8] it is necessary to examine the impact of labor-intensive investment on the birth rate. One widely accepted population growth theory is that rising living standards are accompanied by changes away from the social and economic values which encourage large families. If this is the case, then there may be little or no conflict between maximizing national income and maximizing per capita income.[9] If labor-intensive investments accomplish the former, then they will also achieve maximum per capita income.

The problem of short- versus long-lived investment has been developing a literature of its own during the past five years.[10] The greatest insight to be gained from this literature is that the short-lived, high-"payoff" investment may well lead to a higher ultimate growth rate, when saving (and reinvestment) from the initial return is accounted for. That is, the early, high output permits early and substantial reinvestment, which may cause a more rapid rate of capital accumulation. The three factors determining whether or not this will result are: how much higher the initial output is, how much earlier this output becomes available, and whether the saving and reinvestment ratio is adversely affected by the short-lived method of production. Labor-intensive investments would generally be the short-lived ones, whereas the labor-saving techniques would involve more durable, capital-intensive investment. If the labor-intensive short-lived investments, with the high initial output, also result in the highest ultimate rate of economic growth, then again there is no conflict between the alternative goals suggested above.

The final goal of employment requires no discussion. It is obvious (other things being equal) that labor-intensive methods will employ more labor than capital-intensive investments.

In summation, the labor-intensive hypothesis has been presented as a "rule of thumb" investment guide, which results in maximum output in the immediate future, which may also bring about the highest ultimate rate of growth, which unifies the potentially conflicting goals of output and employment, and offers the possibility at least of having side effects favorable to a lower birth rate. Several other advantages have been attributed to this type of investment which make it particularly appealing to political scientists and sociologists. Labor-intensive usually means small-scale investment, which permits the decentralization of economic power, and consequently a broader-based and more equally distributed political power. Further, small-scale industries can be geographically decentralized, which will minimize or eliminate urban industrial slums.

If there is one country to which the labor-intensive hypothesis should apply, it is India. At this point, therefore, before discussing the theoretical weaknesses of this hypothesis, it will be enlightening to examine the allocation of investment funds during the Indian First Five Year Plan. The main features are presented in Table II. The total investment in manufacturing, including

TABLE II.
ALLOCATION OF GROSS INVESTMENT IN INDIA, 1951-56

Sector	Capital-intensive		Labor-intensive		Total Investment (Rs. Billion)
	(Rs. Billion)	%	(Rs. Billion)	%	
Manufacturing	2.6	21	9.5	79	12.1
Social Overhead	28.2	94	1.7	6	29.9
Agriculture	2.7	17	13.1	83	15.8
Social Services	....	....	1.7	100	1.7
TOTALS	33.5	56%	26.0	44%	59.5

The figures in this table are based on material in the following sources: (1) W. Malenbaum, "India and China: Contrasts in Development Performance," *American Economic Review,* Vol. XLIX, No. 3 (June, 1959), p. 300. (2) W. Malenbaum, *East and West in India's Development* (Washington: National Planning Association, 1959), p. 28. (3) V. V. Bhatt, "Savings and Capital Formation," *Economic Development and Cultural Change,* Vol. VII, No. 3, Part I (April, 1959), pp. 320-332. (4) Twelve reports of the Government of India, the most important being one by The Planning Commission, *Review of the First Five Year Plan* (Delhi, 1957).

the handicraft cottage industries, was Rs. 12.1 billion for the five-year period. Of this Rs. 2.6 billion, or 21%, was invested in very capital-intensive industries (having a capital-labor ratio of Rs. 11,000 per worker, or above), most of which were capital goods industries, such as steel, automobiles, and cement. Rs. 9.5 billion, 79%,was invested in relatively labor-intensive industries (with a capital-labor ratio of Rs. 6,000 per worker, or below), most of which were consumer-goods industries, such as cotton textiles, jute, and sugar. Perhaps even more significant than the substantial emphasis on the capital-intensive industries is the fact that within the labor-intensive industries, investment was often not in the more labor-intensive, hand methods of production, but in the relatively labor-saving, capital-intensive techniques. In jute, for example, the gross investment was Rs. 150 million, primarily for replacement and modernization. This investment was highly labor-saving as is indicated by a 10% drop in employment during the plan period, when output increased 28%.[11] Throughout the First Five Year Plan, the managers of cotton textile mills wanted to introduce automatic looms. Only 8,300 were imported, but more would have been obtained, had not government restrictions and an ultimate ban been imposed.[12] (This ban was to prevent unemployment of the handloom workers.)

In the social overhead industries of power, transport, communications, and housing, total investment was Rs. 29.9 billion. Although capital-labor ratios are not available, qualitative information indicates that 88% was relatively capital-intensive investment in power, telegraph and telephone centers and lines, railways, shipping, ports and harbors, civil air transport, and housing. The remaining 12% was in roads (Rs. 1.5 billion) and in private transport (Rs. 2 billion). Roads can be built by relatively labor-intensive methods, but they may be a capital-intensive method of providing transportation. If unsurfaced roads, requiring labor-intensive maintenance, are built instead of durable, surfaced roads, then the provision of road service would be relatively labor-intensive. Adequate figures are not available, but it may be estimated that about half of the road expenditure was for unsurfaced roads of this kind. Assuming that about half of the private transport investment was in labor-intensive methods, the breakdown of social overhead investments is as follows: 94% capital-intensive; 6% labor-intensive.

The total investment in agriculture was Rs. 15.8 billion. Rs. 1.8 billion (about 11%) was spent for a miscellany of agricultural programs, including land reclamation, fertilizers, and community development. There is a similarity here to the consumer goods investment, in that these agriculture programs may be considered labor-intensive in relation to the capital goods industries, but within many of these programs the labor-intensive methods were stressed less than the more capital-intensive techniques: tractors for land reclamation; chemical fertilizers, instead of urban and rural composts; power fishing vessels, etc. The capital-intensity of irrigation parallels that of roads: if irrigation is by bunds, embankments, canals, channels, and wells, more labor-intensive maintenance is required, and thus these are more labor-intensive methods of irrigation than that provided by durable installations, such as modern high dams. If the labor-intensive "rule of thumb" had been followed, the major irrigation expenditure would have been in the small-scale operations. Of the Rs. 4.1 billion spent on irrigation, only Rs. 1.4 billion was for the small-scale, and Rs. 2.7 billion for the capital-intensive methods. Rs. 10 billion of private investment in agriculture is assumed to be labor-intensive. Consequently, for agriculture as a whole, 83% of the investment was labor-intensive, 17% capital-intensive.

The remainder of the expenditure under the First Five Year Plan was Rs. 1.7 billion for relatively labor-intensive social services and miscellaneous items. Of the total capital expenditures during the Five Year Plan, 56% was in relatively capital-intensive investments. The remaining 44%, while in relatively labor-intensive industries, was often not invested in the *most* labor-intensive techniques available.*

It is possible to react to these findings in two ways: one can hold to the labor-intensive hypothesis, and ask why Indian investment was misallocated; or one can discard the hypothesis, and seek a more meaningful alternative. In spite of the great appeal of the labor-intensive "rule," most economists have followed the latter course. The "rule" has been attacked on two grounds: first, it produces grossly misleading advice as to the allocation of investment *among industries*; and second, concerning the *choice of technique within an industry,* its guidance is at best confusing, and quite often incorrect. The remainder of this paper will analyze, in order, these two criticisms.

A fundamental error in the labor-intensive hypothesis can

---

*This conclusion is supported by an intensive study of five Indian industries by G. Rosen in *Industrial Change in India* (Glencoe, Ill.: The Free Press, 1958). His results indicate "a trend toward rising capital-labor coefficients in the Second Plan which lends support to the conclusion, presented in the previous two chapters, of rising capital-output ratios. The upward trends of both relationships clearly indicate a gradual introduction of labor-saving equipment" (p. 143).

best be brought to light by the following question: In a completely closed economy, with no international trade, should investment be made only in those industries which are most labor-intensive? Without international trade, consumption is necessarily limited to those goods that are produced domestically, and there may exist consumer demands for goods which have only capital-intensive production methods.

If rice can be produced more labor-intensively than cloth, does this mean that all investment should go into rice and none into cloth? If economic growth is to be in any way related to rising living standards and consumer welfare, then the composition of output must be closely related to the pattern of goods that consumers want. Thus, if consumers demand more rice and more cloth, investment should be allocated to the production of both goods regardless of their capital-labor ratios.* An extreme case, which may point up the criticism more clearly, is this: If consumers demand electricity or want any good or service requiring electricity, then some of the limited investment funds should be allocated to a power industry, even though the capital-labor ratio may be very high.

During the past decade, several alternative theories have been formulated to deal with this problem of the allocation of investment funds among industries. The most comprehensive has come to be known as the principle of "balanced growth." [13] The basic notion is a simple one: Investment should be so allocated that the resultant increase in output of each of the various goods coincides with the increased demand for these goods. The fundamental division between investment in consumer goods industries and capital goods industries is determined by the proportion of income which is consumed and saved. Within the consumer goods

*This is not to say that the capital-labor ratios do not have some effect on the quantity of the two goods which consumers will demand. If capital is expensive and labor is cheap, then the labor-intensive good will have a lower price; the quantity demanded will be greater, and thus the investment required in this industry may be greater. The capital-intensive good will be more expensive, but if at this higher price consumers still demand some quantity, then some investment should be allocated to the production of this good. In a free market economy, the profit motive operating through the price system would tend to bring about the proper investment allocation between the two goods.

sector, investment allocation is determined by the proportions in which goods are demanded. A properly working price system, operating in a relatively free market, will approximate the conditions of balanced growth. But lack of the appropriate institutional arrangements for a free market in most underdeveloped areas may result in the necessity of government planning to bring about the balanced growth of output that is desirable.

The balanced growth principle, however, implies that investment should proceed simultaneously on all fronts; that is, all industries are equally important. It ignores or denies the existence of certain priority industries which have a key role to play in economic development. It may not properly take account of "external economies" which accompany certain types of investments. An investment in a multipurpose dam project, for example, may not be profitable in terms of the revenue it receives from marketing its services, but it may have many indirect social benefits in terms of flood control, river navigation, and the growth of industries based on the water or power supply. The sum of the direct and indirect benefits is the important measure by which investments should be compared and the appropriate ones selected. But whereas economists can define this sum conceptually, and they have a name for it (social marginal product), they find it almost impossible, when confronted with the development problem in a given country, to present a comprehensive list of investments which require priority because they have the highest social marginal product.[14]

The reason for this difficulty is quite obvious. The more indirect and abstract the benefits are, the harder it is to discover and quantify them for comparison purposes. The value of an investment in steel may be quite direct and measurable, but can the same be said of education expenditure? Education that increases human skills and productivity is a rather direct investment, although even this presents valuation and measurement problems. But what about the role of education in creating new attitudes and ways of thinking which encourage economic growth? What of the importance of education in bringing about institutional changes, which break with tradition, instill new aspirations, and facilitate the acceptance of innovations and change? The benefits of education may greatly surpass those of the steel mill, but the former are intangible, the latter tangible and easily comprehended.

A partial solution to this dilemma is that these priority investments (or "growing points," as Kindleberger calls them)[15] can be selected by skilled individuals on the basis of qualitative information. For example, there is substantial agreement among experts that underdeveloped areas should stress social overhead investments.[16] In light of this consensus, the allocation of Indian investment (Table II) appears to be quite good: almost 50% of the investment was in this category. (When housing is deducted, however, the allocation appears in a less favorable light: one-fifth of the total investment, about Rs. 12 billion, was in the social overheads of transport, communication, and power.)

Unfortunately, experts do not always agree, as is evident from the vigorous debate over the Indian Second Five Year Plan. The First Plan stressed overheads and agriculture. Although the Second Plan has allocated more spending to all categories, there has been a significant increase in emphasis on manufacturing industry. This increase in planned expenditure on manufacturing was divided as follows: heavy machinery and steel in the capital goods sector, and very labor-intensive cottage industries in the consumer goods sector. Indian officials believe that unemployment is "the most pressing" economic problem,[17] and cottage handicraft industries are one solution. The heavy industry investment is a reflection of the Planning Commission's position that this industry is a key "growing point"; with this emphasis the Indians are moving somewhat toward the Chinese and Russian examples.

Disagreement exists with both aspects of the industrial program. The cottage industry expenditure is criticised on the grounds that the unemployed should be producing capital goods, not placed in make-work projects with inefficient techniques in the consumer goods sector.[18] The stress on heavy capital goods has also been attacked. In an article reviewing the Second Plan, Ragnar Nurkse strongly criticises it, suggesting that the highest priority is still in transport, communications, power, and education. In particular, he believes that the Indian Plans have essentially overlooked the great contribution that education can make. [19]

What, then, is the conclusion concerning the allocation of investment among industries? The labor-intensive rule clearly is not appropriate. Balanced growth provides a useful general framework, which may serve as a guide for much of the investment (this was essentially the basis for the First and Second Five Year Plans), but it omits priorities. The social marginal product of each investment is the appropriate measure of its value and, consequently, is conceptually the best investment guide.* But this is a formal concept, which is difficult to use because precise measurement is impossible. Expert qualitative judgment is called for, but experts may disagree. There is no simple solution. Although the social marginal product appears to be the best, it is far from ideal.

The second criticism of the labor-intensive hypothesis is concerned with the choice of technique within an industry. The validity of the labor-intensive hypothesis depends on whether output will be highest when labor-intensive methods are employed. As noted above, the principle of diminishing returns was the fundamental rationale underlying the output conclusions reached. This principle also notes that "as additional laborers are added to a given quantity of capital, *eventually* a point is reached beyond which total output falls." Table III illustrates the point

TABLE III.

COUNTRY A:	CAPITAL STOCK:	$10	
	POPULATION (LABOR FORCE)	10 MEN	
	Technique 1	Technique 2	Technique 3
1. Capital-labor ratio	$10/1	$10/10 or $1/1	$10/5 or $2/1
2. Total output	$5.00	$10.00	$15.00
3. Output per capita	$ .50	$ 1.00	$ 1.50
4. Capital-output ratio	$2/1	$ 1/1	$ .75/1

*Galenson and Leibenstein, *op. cit.*, and Eckstein, *op. cit.*, have pointed out two weaknesses of the social marginal product (SMP) criterion: it does not reflect differing saving (and reinvestment) rates or differing population growth rates resulting from alternative investments. Thus the technique with the highest SMP may not produce the most valuable per capita consumption pattern. The marginal per capita reinvestment quotient and the marginal growth contribution (the two criteria suggested by these economists) are theoretically better than SMP, but would be even more difficult (if not impossible) to employ at the practical level. As a "rule of thumb" investment guide, SMP, though imperfect, is the best criterion.

I wish to make. Country A is now assumed to have three possible methods of production: Techniques 1 and 2 are the same as before, but now Technique 3 has been discovered which has a capital-labor ratio of $2/1 (ten dollars of capital employs five men) and produces an output of fifteen dollars. Technique 3 is more capital-intensive than Technique 2; that is, the capital-labor ratio is $2/1, instead of $1/1, but it results in a higher total output and a higher output per capita of $1.50 (Line 3). In other words, Technique 2 is inefficient. It is at this point that the labor-intensive hypothesis has received the most criticism, and justly so. The most labor-intensive method may be an inefficient one which results in a lower output, even though more labor has been applied to a given amount of capital. This, apparently, is the plight of many of the handicrafts in India. Technical innovations have occurred in the spinning of yarn, for example, which make hand spinning inefficient.

Because labor-intensive methods may be inefficient, some imprecision and confusion has occurred in the past; this can be avoided by utilizing the capital-output ratio as a measure of capital-intensity rather than the capital-labor ratio.[20] For example, Table III, Line 4, shows the capital-output ratios of the three techniques. Given the capital stock of ten dollars, the lowest capital-output ratio is that of Technique 3, .75. Technique 2 yields a lower output per unit of capital, so has a higher capital-output ratio of 1.0. If labor is plentiful (literally redundant) and capital is the only scarce factor of production, the appropriate investment "rule of thumb" is the "low-capital-output rule"; investment within an industry should be in those techniques with the lowest capital-output ratios.*

The selection of relatively capital-intensive techniques in India during the First Plan makes some sense in terms of the low capital-output rule, whereas it seems totally inappropriate when judged by the labor-intensive hypothesis. Within most capital goods industries, technical choices are limited; labor-intensive methods do not exist. If steel is to be produced (on social mar-

---

*Chenery, op. cit., p. 87, has stated: "The turnover rate [capital-output ratio] is particularly useful in choosing among projects within a given sector." However, the low capital-output criterion has the same two weaknesses as SMP (noted above).

ginal product grounds), then even the technique that has the lowest capital-output ratio may be quite capital-intensive when compared with techniques in other industries. In the consumer goods industries, a range of alternative techniques exists, but apparently in many cases the most labor-intensive are inefficient (as is true of yarn spinning). In terms of the market this means that the handicraft workers are being driven out by the lower prices and superior quality of the products from small and large factories.

The simplicity and yet the generality of the labor-intensive hypothesis for investment allocation have made it very attractive to those concerned with economic growth in the underdeveloped, overpopulated countries of the world. This thesis has been examined in the light of the Indian experience from 1951-56, and has been found to be very weak; it is not adequate as a guide for the proper allocation of investment among industries or for the choice of techniques within an industry. The labor-intensive criterion should be discarded and greater emphasis placed on the alternative criteria, discussed above, which have theoretical validity and yield substantial insight into past experience.

NOTES

1. Many sources could be cited, but the following are typical: Government of India, *Second Five Year Plan* (Delhi, 1956), p. 25; and W. A. Lewis, *The Theory of Economic Growth* (Homewood, Ill.: Irwin, 1955), p. 137.

2. See, for example, N. S. Buchanan, *International Investment and Domestic Welfare* (New York, 1945), p. 24; and H. B. Chenery, "The Application of Investment Criteria," *Quarterly Journal of Economics,* Vol. LXVII, No. 1 (February, 1953), 87.

3. A. E. Kahn, "Investment Criteria in Development Programs," *Quarterly Journal of Economics,* Vol. LXV, No. 1 (February, 1951), 39.

4. W. Galenson and H. Leibenstein, "Investment Criteria, Productivity, and Economic Development," *Quarterly Journal of Economics,* Vol. LXIX, No. 3 (August, 1955), 351-352.

5. O. Eckstein, "Investment Criteria for Economic Development and the Theory of Intertemporal Welfare Economics," *Quarterly Journal of Economics,* Vol. LXXI, No. 1 (February, 1957), 69.

6. J. K. Galbraith, *The Affluent Society* (Boston: Houghton Mifflin, 1958), pp. 7-20.

7. H. J. Bruton, "Growth Models and Underdeveloped Economies," *Journal of Political Economy,* Vol. LXIII (August, 1955), 327.

8. However, Galenson and Leibenstein, *op. cit.,* seem to advocate an increase in the death rate, as was pointed out by J. Moes, "Investment Criteria,

Productivity, and Economic Development: Comment," *Quarterly Journal of Economics*, Vol. LXXI, No. 1 (February, 1957), 163.

9. The impact on population resulting from a given investment allocation is a highly speculative and complicated matter. For alternative formulations of this problem, see Galenson and Leibenstein, *op. cit.*, and S. Enke. "Speculations on Population Growth and Economic Development," *Quarterly Journal of Economics*, Vol. LXXI, No. 1 (February, 1957), 19-35.

10. A few of the articles pertaining to this issue are: E. Domar, "Depreciation, Replacement, and Growth," *Economic Journal*, Vol. LXIII (March, 1953), 1-32; Galenson and Leibenstein, *op. cit.*; P. S. Thomas, "Capital Intensity of Investment and the Economic Development of India," *Papers of the Michigan Academy of Science, Arts, and Letters*, Vol. XLIII (1958), 203-222; R. C. Blitz, "Capital Longevity and Economic Development," *The American Economic Review*, Vol. XLVIII, No. 3 (June, 1958), 313-329.

11. Government of India, Planning Commission, *Programmes of Industrial Development* (Delhi, 1956), pp. 350-356.

12. *Ibid.*, p. 338.

13. There is a vast and growing literature on balanced growth. Perhaps the key source is R. Nurkse, *Problems of Capital Formation in Underdeveloped Countries* (Oxford, 1953).

14. Chenery, *op. cit.*, has made an excellent attempt at such a ranking for Italy.

15. C. P. Kindleberger, *Economic Development* (New York, 1958), p. 161.

16. See Lewis, *op. cit.*, p. 265; R. Nurkse, "Reflections on India's Development Plan," *Quarterly Journal of Economics*, Vol. LXXI, No. 2 (May, 1957), 188-204; and Kindleberger, *op. cit.*, pp. 161, 167.

17. Nurkse, "Reflections . . . ," p. 188.

18. C. N. Vakil and P. R. Brahmanand, *Planning for an Expanding Economy* (Bombay, 1956), pp. 248-249.

19. Nurkse, "Reflections . . . ," p. 199.

20. For a more detailed discussion of the capital-output ratio, and some examples of the confusion surrounding the capital-labor ratio, see Thomas, *op. cit.*

The Anatomy of an Ideology: Japanese Imperialism

RALPH M. MIWA
University of Missouri

The Japanese ideology for imperialism has been dismissed in the past by some as mere rationalizations for the pursuit of national self-interest. At other times, researchers have approached the subject from the standpoint of morality and held Japanese imperialism to be inconsonant with certain fundamental moral precepts.

It has been argued in turn that both of these orientations have implicitly assumed the values of Western civilization and have, consequently, subjected the Japanese ideology to a judgement based primarily upon Western values. It has also been argued, however, that this is a form of ethnocentrism not to be particularly praised or deprecated because it is an inevitability due to the limits imposed by a particular cultural milieu; that people perforce judge upon the basis of their own environment and experience. Individuals expressing this opinion seem to have tacitly assumed that no one can ever hope to pass critical judgement upon the actions of others.

Proponents of such a point of view fail to understand that in studying the development of an ideology which has led a nation to choose a particular course of action, we may criticize and analyze the ideology by inquiring into the consistency of premises with conclusions and by comparing assumed facts in the ideology with discoverable facts in history. In this way, it is conceivable that we can examine the ideology of imperialism in its own milieu and yet be able to arrive at a reasonably objective judgement. We may argue with the imperialist, not upon the merits of his values or our values, but upon the premises and causes he stipulates himself. Karl Mannheim's methodological lessons, in this regard, are significant.

The ideology of Japanese imperialism, especially at the turn of the twentieth century, was framed in terms of a reaction against so-called Western colonization and expansion in Asia. Towards the 1930's, and especially just prior to 1941, Japanese exhortations turned from the theory of divine revelations as the basis of expansionism propounded by Toyotomi Hideyoshi and the jingoistic nationalism urged by Yoshida Shoin and Hashimoto Sanai, to a curious blending of economic dialectics and nationalism not radically different from Marxist-Leninist concepts. There occurred in Japanese thought the idea that the only way to compete successfully in a twentieth-century world economy marked by colonial expansionism and quests for sources of raw materials was to pursue a program of military conquests.

With the advent of Admiral Sekine, General Doihara, and the Imperial Rescript of 1941, Japanese expansionist rationale developed this proto-Marxist line of explanation and theoretical justification. For example, Sekine referred to the contradiction of capitalism as practiced by Great Britain wherein she sought to extract raw materials from subjugated territories, preventing industrialization because of its competitive potential, thus impoverishing them, and then attempting to make of them markets for her manufactured goods, a process which meant that Britain could not practice democracy abroad while professing to be its champion at home. Of course, argued Sekine, Japan hoped to halt this process which otherwise would drive her to "stagnancy" and "daily impoverishment." Japan's New Order meant one in which "no nation is to exploit other nations." The alternative package deal for what he called the "exploiting system" was a system of mutual trade and industrialization. The Far East, under Japan's "benevolent guidance," had to lift itself by its own economic bootstraps.[1]

Reiterating the Sekine argument against Western methods of colonization, Doihara played upon the theme of Asia for the Asians. A variation of the theme occurred in the idea that an essential difference existed between Western and Japanese hegemony. The former was motivated purely by self-interest, whereas the latter was fundamentally concerned with Asiatic control over its own affairs. The mantle cloaking the Japanese social service system was to be benevolent paternalism.[2]

The Imperial Rescript of 1941 issued by Emperor Hirohito proclaimed that the eighteenth-century Industrial Revolution in Europe demanded increased sources of raw materials and consequent overseas markets for the disposal of manufactured goods. These two needs led to competition for the acquisition of colonies and the doctrine of the survival of the fittest which "gradually enlarged its inconsistency and culminated in the outbreak of the World War of 1914." After victory, Britain, France, and the United States proceeded to dominate Europe, exploiting areas in self-interest. The rise of Japan as an industrial power after 1918 was viewed unfavorably by the same Western powers who were intent on dominating East Asia themselves. Japan was forced to be the object of retaliatory actions in the form of economic pressure, diplomatic opposition, and propaganda.[3]

Contemporary Japanese government officials, economists, and foreign service career personnel such as Arita Hachiro, Takahashi Kamekichi, Kawashima Nobutaro, Sayegusa Shigetomo, Shiratori Toshio, and others pursued a similar argument up to 1941. Arita was the group's most eloquent ideological polemicist. He declared that Great Britian and the United States were "free-traders" only so long as they possessed an overpowering technological advantage in the process of industrialization. Once the gap narrowed, Arita said, "They promptly abandoned the principles of Adam Smith which had been held dear for a hundred years." They then proceeded to adopt a protective trade policy contrary to the principles they had advocated for other countries. Arita concluded that Japanese efforts to develop into a strong power were but the "natural outcome of the action of the Great Powers themselves, which having both abundant raw materials and thriving markets, have tended to drive these countries to extinction by their exclusion policies both political and economic."[4]

Kada Tatsuji and Matsuoka Yosuke, as spokesmen for the concept of greater East Asia, repeated much of the rationale. The outstanding characteristic of their approach may be seen in the emphasis placed upon the uncontrollable elements of time and fate. As a consequence, the rationale resembled Marxist-Leninist thinking more closely than any of the predecessors. But whereas Marx and his ideological sympathizers used the thesis to argue that imperialism was the inevitable resultant of monopoly capitalism, the Japanese polemicists adopted it in defense of their own imperialistic ambitions. The manner in which this paradoxical process occurred is of the greatest significance, and it is important to understand this in analyzing Japanese problems.

Since much of the theses propounded by Kada and Matsuoka were basically similar, they will be combined for the purposes of this discussion.[5]

The thesis was argued that Japan was forced out of her policy of seclusion by a display of armed strength on the part of the West, specifically the United States. After being compelled to enter the world industrial complex, Japan found herself obstructed by numerous handicaps.

First, America, then Britain, France, and Russia, demanded extraterritorial rights and a low customs tariff by treaty. This represented the imperialistic formula which had everywhere marked Western penetration into the East, said Kada and Matsuoka. Through these means, they continued, Eastern Asia was reduced to colonial or semicolonial status. Fortunately, Japan escaped the worst that had befallen other countries of the East. But this was only because of Japan's comparatively advanced stage, and she was not much better off, the rationale continued.

Second, the thesis claimed that Japan was forced to fight for every concession that meant freedom from the disadvantages imposed by her late arrival into the world's arena of competitive industrialism. In addition to the technological advances enjoyed, these Western powers had completely staked out the areas of natural resources and of markets. In order to develop herself politically and economically, and in order to survive in the competitive world complex, Japan "proceeded to take a leaf" from the Western guide to imperialism. In Japan's early stages she merely emulated that which had been the accepted formula in the West. But at every turn, Japan found obstacles.

Third, the rationale claimed that Japan was forced to compete in a world complex of industrialism which arbitrarily placed her in a position where the Japanese economy had to be geared to the rest of the world economy. But owing to monopolistic practices growing out of so-called "nationalistic economies," Japan had to produce goods and articles primarily for the export trade. Specialization for survival in agriculture and industry came to be the dominant policy. Because of her small and restricted territory, and due to her dearth of raw materials, Japan became economically subservient to the nations of the West. In order to escape from this state of affairs, Japan had to secure access to raw-material areas which would not be subject to the political sanctions of competing powers. Furthermore, it was claimed, Japan's unprecedented population increase made imperative a solution of this dilemma induced in the first instance by the world monopolies.

Fourth, the West's imperialistic formula, which laid stress on exploitation purely for profit without regard to the co-prosperity and mutual security of the colonized areas, was anachronistic. It failed to consider the welfare of the peoples of the colonial areas. Japan's plan for a Greater East Asia envisaged the political and economic well-being of all the peoples of the area, not just the enterprise nation, continued the rationale. Kada and Matsuoka claimed that the West ostensibly preached democracy but practiced something more akin to pure exploitation; and Japan aimed to correct these inequities by implementing her new doctrine.

This theory formed the thesis of the argument presented by Kada, Matsuoka, and the rest of the publicists. The strong proto-Marxist undertones may be perceived throughout the formulation of the rationale.

There were other minor theses presented during the course of the development of the doctrine of a Co-Prosperity Sphere by the publicists. These are enumerated in the following paragraphs.

(1) The common Asian consciousness of racial homogeneity and the fact of geographical propinquity among Asian countries made more plausible the concept and formation of an East Asian Co-Prosperity Sphere.

(2) The West desired Japan's weakening by a war of attrition in China. The West also wanted Japan's elimination as a force likely to disrupt the status quo of colonial powers in Asia. Western aid to the Chinese, therefore, was really an investment in the continuation of Western imperialism.

(3) Soviet Communism was a disintegrative influence and had

to be combated. It was held to be absolutely incompatible with both the civilization and "intrinsic racial characteristics" of the Eastern peoples. Thus, East Asia had to form an alliance for defense.

(4) The Japanese were aware of the distinctive characteristics of Asiatic ethnology, and consequently were best prepared to achieve complete "racial unity." Japan's familiarity with the peculiarities of history, geography, and cultural conditions in East Asia enabled her, for example, to weld such a heterogeneous country as Manchuria into a homogeneous entity called Manchukuo. This fact amply qualified her for the new undertaking.

The other publicists generally adhered to these themes. The material has been presented to indicate the consistency and persistency of certain underlying themes in the Japanese rationale. There is, however, one significant point which is present in the argument urged by Arita and Sayegusa. It is a variation of the inner contradiction of monopoly capital argument used against Western nations by the other publicists.[6]

Arita opened the first volley by asserting that for a hundred years up to 1900, Adam Smith was the ideological protagonist of the West. Countries contravening his precepts were "ostracized" and forced to open their doors to Western trade. However, Eastern development in political and economic matters was retarded by this action by the more advanced countries. Political and economic pressures were brought to bear against East Asian countries. The Western nations suppressed political and economic development in Asia because they were not in the West's own best interests.

With the passage of time, nations such as Great Britain and the United States realized that their industrial power could not prevent further progress on the part of these newly risen nations. When they became aware of this fact, both Great Britain and the United States promptly discarded the principle of free trade and adopted a prohibitive trade policy exemplified in customs barriers, tariffs, preferential treatment, etc. The next effect of this sudden *volte-face* of principle was only a natural outcome. It resulted in the attempt on the part of nations, such as Japan, to form self-sufficient economic spheres free from Western power and influence. The Western powers themselves started the in-

evitable reaction by the imposition of exclusion policies to protect their monopoly of raw materials and thriving markets.

Sayegusa commented in conclusion that it was ironic when
those who professed to be the defenders of democratic ways had
no alternative but to emulate totalitarianism.

As far as the official rationale of the Japanese government was
concerned, it embodied practically every theoretical argument
that has been surveyed. The official East Asia Co-Prosperity
Sphere doctrine repeated the entire devious course of Japanese
thought on imperialism. Western capitalism was identified with
Western imperialism and a thirst for exploitation. Colonialism
by the West meant utter disregard for the peoples of the East.
Ironically, these arguments were being pressed incessantly and
vehemently by a nation which had set as its unalterable goal an
imperialistic empire encompassing the whole of East Asia.[7]

Study of the Japanese ideology for imperialism may be significant because it illustrates the tremendous psychological attraction
of a thesis which plays upon the *felt* inequities and injustices of
a system and a situation which seemed to have reacted unfavorably to the best interests of certain groups of people. The ideology combines symbols which cater to the collective paranoia of
both the extreme left and the right so as to make a serious study
of its growth and development a necessity. This is an age which
is characterized by appeals to mass emotion and the currying of
political sentiment, both fundamentally based upon a sense of
realpolitik which recognizes that paranoia can be manipulated
for whatever ends the manipulator may decree.

Rationalizations for the type of expansionism displayed by
Japan have sometimes been cavalierly discounted as mere propaganda. This explanation does not take into account the consistency of certain economic premises. Nor does it explain the
persistence of the similarity with over-all proto-Marxist ideological arguments. But most important of all, it fails to concede that
a rationale may be attractive to the general public because it
accords well with the public temperament. The crucial question
which arises from serious study of the Japanese ideology seems to
be: What factors might there have been which led the people to
develop the sort of thinking which led to easy acceptance of the
rationale? A secondary, but by no means unimportant, related

question may be: What element of truth did the rationale contain which may have provided that degree of plausibility needed to sell the doctrine?

This approach provides a method which may be used to study the disparate facts and phenomena of Japanese aggression more meaningfully. Moreover, by the same tool, insight may be gained as to the "truth" that the Japanese "propagandists" withheld in order to achieve the desired result. It would be a tenuous argument to hold that the general currency given the rationale meant it was a valid reflection of the actual economic and political situation in Japan. The collusion in Japan between certain economic forces and the military in the subsequent imperialistic ventures makes one skeptical. In studying the pattern of the rationale, perhaps the card that was held back may be disclosed.

Organizations such as the Sekka Bōshidan (Anti-Communist League), which inveighed the *zaibatsu* influences, such as Mitsui, to consider carefully the effects of their monopoly program, must be carefully analyzed. Radical thoughts in sympathy with Soviet revolutionary theories had been noticeable in their increase. The labor movement in particular became infected with the bacillus of Marxism. This was all happening from the end of World War I to the twenties when monopoly capital controlled, directly or indirectly, 75 percent of the total corporate wealth of Japan.

It should be emphasized that organizations such as the Sekka Bōshidan were essentially rightist movements—but swayed enough by the warnings of catastrophe apparent in the alliance of revolutionary proto-Marxist ideology and the various dissatisfied elements amongst both the unemployed urban workers and agricultural elements to heed seriously the dangers of runaway monopoly capitalism.

First and always nationalistic, rightist organizations such as the Sekka Bōshidan rallied against the momentum being generated by the body of insecure agriculture and labor elements. By 1925, this combination of farmers and urban proletariat had become a serious threat to the continued security of the existing *zaibatsu* interests. In attempting to stem this tide, the *zaibatsu* cultivated the friendship of the extreme right-wing groups at first. The bond reinforcing this relationship was the mutual distrust of international communism. When the position of the *zaibatsu* became still more critical, the monopoly capitalists were forced to align themselves with the most influential and articulate segment of this rightist movement, the military.

It was this combination, composed of extremist military elements and an intimidated *zaibatsu*, which snatched the reins of government from the political parties. It was not a group, as sometimes supposed by dogmatic adherents of Marxism, composed only of dissatisfied young officers deeply in sympathy with the peasant-proletariat aspect of the class struggle. But the government was placed in a position where the interests of agricultural and labor elements had to be placated. This was done by means of improving the financial status of small producers and controlling the *zaibatsu* operations.[8] However, the increasing prosperity in foreign trade and the demand for Japanese goods brought about independence of action on the part of the *zaibatsu*. These interests were temporarily in a position to pursue a less obsequious course, as subordinate partners in an unholy alliance, striking a balance between becoming prosperous and making concessions. But as the series of assassinations grew, including that of Baron Dan of Mitsui, that economic and political tightrope walking was stopped. Disciplinary measures were enforced, but the consequence was a further growth in the influence of the military. The government, again, had to accede further to the demands of the dissatisfied elements.[9]

This phase of the rise of Japanese totalitarianism is central to the understanding of both the ideology of imperialism and the structure of the government which began more vehement espousals of the doctrine.

In general, all these manifestations of insecurity were a reflection of the economic conditions of the times during the late twenties. During this particular span, Japan's foreign trade had suffered a 50 percent decrease, farm income had gone down a third, and agricultural and industrial debts were more than the combined national income. While wages were being decreased, conflicts between tenants and landlords, and industrial workers and industry were on the increase. The public was dissatisfied with the government. The country was faced with imminent depression. Unemployment began to show perceptible increases. This was especially so in the case of salaried workers.

The *zaibatsu* organizations had retreated under the heavy pressure brought to bear on their activities. *Mitsui* especially sought to escape public abuse. Shifts in management personnel were made to accommodate the new prevailing public attitude towards large financial and industrial corporations. Announcement was made that *Mitsui* would contract its scope of business, withdrawing from production of minor agricultural products. Moves were made to begin the sale of large holdings of shares in the more lucrative monopolies such as the Oji Paper Company. In 1932, the corporation remitted three million yen to be used to alleviate economic distress caused by trade dislocations. This was followed in 1933 by the establishment of a thirty million yen endowment fund for the purposes of furthering academic research in the social services.[10] To add to public resentment caused by such *zaibatsu* machinations as profit seeking through increased dollar purchases, the political parties were exposed as corrupt partners of the economic combines. Exposé after exposé undermined the confidence of the people in party government, which since the turn of the decade had been slowly attaining prestige.

The ideological fervor of the times on the part of the dissident Army faction may be gathered from the following, which purports to be a translation of a leaflet of the National Federation of Young Officers:

> The Japanese army and navy, bound body and soul to the people, and to the tradition of Bushidō, see with indignation the influence of commercial speculative circles growing to the detriment of national patriotism. The political parties, a common enemy of the nation, should be destroyed. The capitalists, with their arbitrary authority, should be killed. Under the leadership of the Emperor, we must restore the true goal of our Empire, and institute the principle of self government.[11]

Although in theory restrained from active political participation by an Imperial Rescript of the Emperor in 1882, the growing number of officer personnel recruited from the farming and urban workers since 1927 became restless under the conservatism of the older Chōshu elements. Stablizing the national livelihood became their paramount ideal, insofar as their exhortations were concerned. Anticapitalism, anticommunism, veneration for the Emperor, and territorial acquisitions became shibboleths for their program of action. This new proletarian element in the conscript army identified the interests of the proletariat with its own. A segment of the older officer class assumed leadership of the faction and came, in time, to assume actual governmental control.[12]

In early 1931, the Japanese Labor, Farm, and Masses Party (Zenkoku-Rōnōtaishu-tō) was formed by dissident groups including farmers and urban workers. The extreme left- and right-wing groups did not participate in its early formation. The party platform included pronouncements which indicated that profound disturbances, not arising from any particular political viewpoint, were troubling the masses of the people.

The Japanese themselves, through spokesmen such as Fujisawa Chikao, sought a way out of the dilemma in which they found themselves. Wallowing haplessly in the unfamiliar morass of Soviet dialectics and Western liberalism, the discontentment expressed itself by flailing against both the institution of capitalism which supposedly contributed to the economic insecurity of the people and the prescription advanced by Marxism to cure its baneful effects. Fujisawa railed against the "sway of capitalism [which] allows only a small and privileged class to spend for comfort and pleasure" and criticized the party politicians who had "denegrated into mouthpieces of the privileged class. . . ." But at the same time, the reluctance of the Japanese to accept communism as a panacea could be seen in the statement: Due to indiscriminate introduction of Occidental capitalism since the Meiji Era, principles disregarding the solidarity of the family have crept unawares into national thought. "As a strong reaction against these capitalistic principles, Marxism has mistakenly been embraced because of its scientific simplicity. . . ." Fujisawa sought salvation in a nebulous "national spirit" which would avoid the divisive effects of both communism and capitalism. This "national spirit," as the West found out eventually, was Imperialism.[13]

Japanese economic recovery from the adverse effects of the twenties and early thirties was frustrated by the military extremists who provoked incidents overseas to secure a tighter rein on government. The Japanese government, which needed a stimulation of foreign trade to counter the military's more spectacular successes in the field, were confronted by foreign trade restrictions. Higher tariffs were placed by foreign countries on quotas, and regulations were affixed whereby Japanese imports into a specified marketing area were permitted only upon condition that a similar volume of exports from the same area was maintained. In order to control the export of goods into these areas and also to prevent the imposition of similar restrictions in other areas, the Export Associations were utilized. These organizations originally had been created to stimulate foreign trade. They had existed as instruments among certain producers to arrive at a self-imposed export quota and price range in order to develop without incurring restrictions in foreign markets. In the post-1933 era, they were used to forestall threatened foreign restrictions by being assigned the responsibility of regulating both volume and price, as before 1933, but this time by government intervention rather than through cooperative self-endeavor. These associations were also charged with the task of evaluating potential foreign market areas in order to find countries where Japan could effect a balanced exchange of raw materials for Japanese industrial goods.[14]

Organizations such as the Nippon Kokumin Shakaitō (Japanese National Socialist Party) and the Nihon Kokka Shakaitō (Japan State Socialist Party) sprang up in this climate permeated with dissatisfaction against the existing form of economy and insecurity as to the future course of Japan. Slogans similar to the type of ideology previously analyzed, such as "Replace the capitalist state by a national administration based on loyalty," "Destroy capitalism and establish Socialism under state control," "Give freedom to the Asiatic nations in accordance with the principles of social equality," were composed and disseminated.

These groups were able to attract urban workers as well as farmer-labor groups by playing upon a basic theme of chauvinism with the cry: "Imperial Rule!" In retrospect, we can see that all the diverse elements of the Greater East Asia Co-Prosperity Sphere doctrine were natural fuel for the furnace of resentment. Capitalistic inefficiency and greed, Western inconsistency in blocking the development of Japan, and democratic hypocrisy in espousal of liberalism, were all attacked to rally the forces of economic insecurity and nationalism. The call for the equitable distribution of natural resources, equality of the Asiatic races, and

the idea of common prosperity in the Orient reflected the ac-
cumulated feeling of frustration.

After the initial successes of the military in the field between
1931 and 1937, the Japanese government and the complex of industrial economy seemed unable to halt the march towards imperialism and war. That portion of the history of Japan has been
seen with stark clarity. However, militarism alone is insufficient
to explain Japanese imperialism. The expansionism of Japan,
and the imperialism of its leaders were also psychotic irrational-
isms which grew out of the complex of economics, politics, and
social movements reacting upon a confused and frustrated people.
To ascribe Japanese imperialism to the archfiend Tojo, or to
paint a picture of it as primarily the work of conspiratorial
societies is simply to involve oneself in tautologies.

Unable to understand the complexities which had contributed
towards the *zaibatsu*-type economy, and chafing under the restrictions imposed by regulatory measures born out of the necessity for competing in a progessively intensified world economy,
the Japanese people as a whole found themselves emotionally
driven to accept the kind of rationale propounded by the im-
perialists. It was comparatively easy for them to attack capitalism
as the source of all evil and to seek a panacea in imperialism
rather than to work out problems internally. The internal restrictive controls, the easy identification of capital accumulations,
were all increasing. But the significant point missed by the adherents and enunciators of imperialism was that such means as
the Export Associations were conceived of as protective and pre-
ventive instruments against the further imposition of obstacles
upon Japanese trade by the West. Foreign tariff barriers and
restrictions against "dumping" practices were increasing overseas
due to the competition engendered by uncontrolled mass production of Japanese goods leading to low prices. Moreover, large-
scale accumulations of capital were advantageous for the tardy
Japanese competitor in the world economy.

Caught in such a situation, the Japanese people were eager
subscribers to the doctrinaire explanation of the polemicists who
essentially followed proto-Marxist-Leninist outlines. The idea of
the "inner inconsistency of Western industrialism" and the many
variations on this central thesis accorded well with the temper of

the times. The fitting together of this rationale, heavily interspersed with chauvinism, was a task made to order for the imperialist rationale. True, Marxist-Leninism did not preach external solutions, such as imperialism, for internal economic problems. *But this is where the whole irony of the ideology of imperialism lies. The Japanese used the basic premises of an ideology, which was originally conceived of as an analysis of why monopoly capitalism would destroy itself by an imperialistic conflict, to argue that insofar as Japan was concerned, she was driven to imperialism by the inequities of the capitalistic system.* In effect, Japanese imperialism embraced Marxist-Leninism for basic elements in the rationale for expansion while seeming to be totally unaware that the communist ideology decried imperialism as the inevitable evil of nations such as Japan. The development of such an ideology in the context of a rapidly industrializing nation such as Japan holds great implications for students of newly emergent nations today.

NOTES

1. Sekine Gunpei, *Dai Tōa (Greater East Asia)* (Tōa Kensetsu Kyōkai, Tokyo, 1937).
2. Doihara Kenji, "Roots of Japan's National Policy towards China," *Chūo Kōron (Central Review,* Tokyo), 1938. See also *Pulse of Japan* (Tokyo: Tokyo Information Bureau, 1938) for similar theses contributed by Arita Hachiro, Kawai Tatsuo, Kaneko Kentaro, Oyama Ujiro, Yamamoto Eisuke, Fujisawa Ryuichi, and Takagi Rokuo. Doihara also referred to population pressure as another cause for the necessity to expand.
3. Donald Tewksbury, *Source Book on Far Eastern Ideologies* (New York, 1949), pp. 170-173.
4. Arita Hachiro, "The Greater East Asian Sphere of Common Prosperity," *Contemporary Japan* (Tokyo), Vol. X, No. 1, p. 39. See also Takahashi Kamekichi, "Economic Significance of East Asiatic Co-Prosperity Sphere," *Contemporary Japan,* Vol. X, No. 1, and Uyeda Teijiro, *The Recent Development of Japanese Foreign Trade with Special Reference to Restrictive Policies of Other Countries and Attempts at Trade Agreements,* Japanese Council Papers No. 3 (Tokyo: Institute of Pacific Relations, 1936).
5. Kada Tetsuji, *Gendai no Shokumin Seisaku (Modern Colonial Policies)* (Tokyo, 1937). See also Kada, "Theory of an East Asiatic Unity," *Contemporary Japan* (Tokyo), 1938. The Japanese Military Press Propaganda Section pursued essentially these same agreements throughout the occupation of the Malayan peninsula in World War II. From issue No. 1, February 20, 1942, to issue No. 851, August 21, 1945, the *Shōnan Shimbun (Malayan Times),* the official organ of the Japanese Command in Southeast Asia, hammered at the theme that the war was directed against Western racism and colonial practices.

6. Sayegusa Shigetomo, "Economic Self-Defense," *Contemporary Japan* (Tokyo), X, No. 3, pp. 281-294.
7. See Statement of the Japanese Government, November 3, 1938, *Documents on American Foreign Relations,* January 1938-June 1939, pp. 229-230. S. Shepard Jones, Denys P. Meyers (Boston, 1939). See Statement of the Japanese Minister for Foreign Affairs [Arita], December 19, 1938, *Japan Weekly Chronicle,* December 22, 1938, p. 734. Quoted Documents pp. 232-236.
8. Chitoshi Yanaga, *Japan since Perry* (New York, 1951). See *Report of United States Commission on Japanese Combines,* United States State Department, Part I (March, 1946). Compromises were reached in many of the programs pushed by organizations such as the National Socialist Party which included limitation of taxes to a graduate income and property tax, state aid to veterans and disabled servicemen, limitation of interest on loans and deposits to three percent, system of state unemployment benefits, bargaining rights of laborers, etc.
9. Minister of Justice Dr. Koyama asserted that he was reluctant to punish the perpetrators of the Inukai assassination because the avowed purport of the act was a patriotic one. Newspapers and publications accorded hero status to some of the assassinators.
10. G. C. Allen, "The Industrialization of Japan and Manchukuo, 1939-40," from Gordon, Allen, and Penrose: *House of Mitsui,* p. 24.
11. O. Tanin and M. Yohan, *Militarism in Japan* (London, 1934), p. 202.
12. For round-table discussion of the development and influence of the Army, see *Nippon no Guntai (The Japanese Army)* by the collaborating authors: Iizuka Koji, Murayama Masao, Minami Hiroshi, Iida Rinzo, Komatsu Genichi, and Toyozaki Shoji (Tokyo, 1951).
13. M. S. Kennedy, "The Reactionary Movement of 1932," *Contemporary Japan,* Vol. 1. See *Nippon Kokka Shugi Undōshi (History of Japanese Nationalist Movements)* (2 vols.; Tokyo, 1952), which deals with Japanese national socialism and its development. The organization and growth of the Japanese labor movement and the nationalist organizations, such as the Dai Nippon Kokutai Shakai (The Association of Japanese Nationalism) and Aikoku Seiji Domei (League of Patriots), are analyzed. The fascist roots, organization, and composition of the participants of the February 26 Incident are thoroughly discussed.
14. G. C. Allen, *Japanese Industry: Its Recent Development and Present Condition* (Institute of Pacific Relations, 1940), pp. 12-13.

On the Place of U Nu's Buddhist Socialism in Burma's History of Ideas

MANUEL SARKISYANZ

Merton-Visiting Professor, Universities of Kiel and Freiburg, West Germany

U Nu's Burma has been studied in a number of works that deal with its political history,[1] its administrative development, economics,[2] sociology,[3] and international relations.[4] While these spheres have been repeatedly treated, relatively little has appeared in either English or Burmese on the intellectual history of modern Burma. On the other hand, the comparative history of ideas indicates the significance of intellectual developments in Burma, as it is the only major area of Theravāda Buddhism to pass through an acute intellectual crisis and collapse of the traditional form of state.

The political implications of its Buddhism seem less comprehensible in the context of the canonical, monastic Buddhism of the Pāli scriptures than in connection with the not so widely known and less monastic Buddhist ethos of medieval Burmese kingship in the tradition of Aśoka, as exemplified in epigraphic

Paper read before the Midwest Conference on Asian Affairs at Norman, Oklahoma, on October 28, 1960. The field research in Burma, on which it is largely based, was made possible by a grant of the Guggenheim Foundation of New York. While in Burma (1959), the writer was benefited by the advice and by the kind assistance of Justice U Chan Htoon of the Supreme Court of the Union of Burma, President of the Buddha Sasana Council. U Wan Nyunt of the United States Educational Foundation Board, Rangoon, has been most helpful in the collection of material in the Burmese language, which would have taken the author very much longer without his assistance. Many other Burmans have assisted with advice and research suggestions or interviews; a full list of personal acknowledgments will be contained in the forthcoming book, *Buddhist Backgrounds of the Burmese Revolution.*

sources, best known from the Pagan period. Thus King Alaung-sithu proclaimed in 1141 the prototype of his aspirations as follows:

> I would build a causeway sheer athwart the river of Saṁsāra,
> And all folk would speed across until they reach the Blessed
>   City.
> I myself would cross and drag the drowning over.
> Ay, myself tamed, I would tame the wilful; comforted, com-
>   fort the timid;
> Wakened, wake the asleep; cooled, cool the burning;
> Freed, set free the bound. Tranquil and led by the good doc-
>   trines
> I would hatred calm. . . .
> Won not by oppression may my wealth remain. . . .
> As the best of men, forsaking worldly fame and worthless
>   wealth,
> Fled, for he saw their meaning.
> So would I, all worldly wealth forsaking, draw me near
> Religion and the threefold course ensue. . . .
> Beholding man's distress, I would put forth my energies,
> And save men, spirits, worlds,
> From seas of endless change. . . .[5]

Thus within Theravāda Buddhism political power over the world of impermanence rationalized itself in terms of the king's exemplary charisma of liberation from this impermanence. Such salvation in the Buddhism of Burma is to be achieved only through individual contemplation and meditation. The corresponding political ideal was the creation of such social conditions as would permit the liberating meditation. Therefore the state was to ensure economic relationships allowing leisure for meditation on which depended the achievement of Nibbāna.[6] This constituted the Buddhist ethos of Burmese kingship, with its ideal of a social order permitting each living being to save himself. Thus King Kyanzitthā of the Pagan Dynasty proclaimed in 1098 or 1099 what we may call his Buddhist ideology of state in the following words:

> Tribhuwanādityadhammarāja, with his right hand he shall give boiled rice and bread to all the people, with his left hand he shall give ornaments and wearing apparel to all men. Men who are not equal in body, speech, or in spirit, the king shall make them equal. . . . Even all the poor old women who sell pots and potlids . . . they shall become rich. . . . Those who

lack cattle shall have plenty of cattle. . . . The pious gifts the
king made in . . . digging tanks or planting groves . . . only in
order that all beings might escape out of Saṁsāra, . . . might
obtain happiness in the worlds beyond until they arrive in
Nirvāṇa. The bar of the gate of Heaven . . . by wisdom shall
the king draw open . . . and shall bring all mankind into
heaven. He shall empty the four painful states of existence.
When the King of the Law shall preach the Law, the sounds
of applause of all men shall be like the sounds of rainstorm at
the end of the year. . . . That all beings may obtain . . . plenty
and be free from famine in every place that lacks water and
land, our lord, the king, digs water tanks, creates cultivation,
. . . the exalted mighty universal monarch, the omniscient one,
the Bodhisattva, who shall verily become the Buddha that
saves and redeems all beings, who is great in compassion for
all beings, who is exalted above all other kings that dwell in
the four quarters of the earth. . . .[7]

Even at its worst in practice, a practice that as often as not meant
ruling with methods of blood and iron, the Burmese monarchy
had preserved to the end of its existence in theory this ethos of
the ruler as "Cakkavatī" and potential Buddha, benefactor and
saviour of all beings. If these ideas have been illustrated above by
examples from the epigraphy of the Pagan period (1044-1287)
and not from the inscriptions of later dynasties, it is firstly because the era of Pagan was the formative period of Burmese culture, and secondly because the inscriptions of its successors have
hardly been systematically published beyond the fourteenth century, let alone edited and made accessible. But the continuity of
these traditions, which were so vivid in medieval Burma, has
been preserved into the twentieth century by Burmese folklore
which is robustly alive among Burma's rural majority and even
affects the cities. A perfect Buddhist ruler, closely associated with
the future Buddha, is the theme of some of Burma's most popular
prophecies, and of one of Burma's most widely read vernacular
books, republished again and again, including an edition in
1955.[8] Although its "Buddha Raja Marvel Prince" apparently is
not mentioned explicitly in the Western literature about Burma,
the belief in him is almost universal among the Burmese people
outside the English-educated minority—and in many cases it is
even found within it. This lore ultimately derives from the Pāli
Dīgha-Nikāya, but has "Burmanized" its Cakkavatī world-ruler

through associations with the last Burmese (Konbaung) dynasty and postwar events. "Sedja Min" is expected to establish a perfect society with inexhaustible wealth for all and to win the whole world for Buddhism.[9] Such utopia is to come at the end of the present world age of degeneration. This cycle of decline began, according to Pāli Buddhist philosophy of history (as exemplified by the Ceylonese Mahāvaṁsa—and the Burmese Manu-Dhamma-that), when the Illusion of the Self led men to the appropriation of the freely growing means of livelihood, originally held in common by all men, as private property, causing the disappearance of the legendary Padeytha-Tree that had supplied all material needs of humanity and making necessary the election of the first ruler, a future Buddha.[10] Thus from Burmese folklore and ultimately from the Buddhist historiography of Ceylon comes the tradition about a perfect utopian society that was thought to have existed at the beginning of time, before men succumbed to the suffering-causing illusion, when property originated from theft and men were obliged to elect a chief executive.

Although with the collapse of the Burmese Kingdom in 1885 Burma's elite turned increasingly away from Burmese traditions and became culturally anglicized to varying degrees, these folk-ideas about a perfect society, its loss, and the consequent origin of political power from the people were transmitted into the ideology of the Burmese Revolution and independence movement by Thakin Kudaw Hmine through his book *Thakin-Tīkā,* a literary glorification of the revolutionary Thakin-Dobama Party.[11] To this eventually victorious independence party (which was organized by English-educated students, and which produced the present ruling statesmen of Burma), Thakin Kudaw Hmine, called "Burma's Rabindranath Tagore," made important ideological contributions from Burmese tradition and Buddhist sources. That such traditionalist elements in "Thakin" ideology have remained practically unnoticed in the Western literature about modern Burma is largely due to their lack of expression in sources in the English language: Thakin Kudaw Hmine does not write in English. This octogenarian poet is a living historical link of the Burmese Revolution with the cultural traditions of pre-British Burma. As a ten-year-old pupil in a Buddhist monastery school he wept bitter tears at the sight of the last Burmese king

being taken away into British captivity (in 1885). At a time, in
the early twentieth century, when Burma's secular elite through
its colonial education had become separated from Burmese culture, had lost touch with Burmese history, and had largely lost
familiarity with literary Burmese as means of written expression,
Kudaw Hmine brought back to the consciousness of the intelligentsia Burma's historical and literary lore.[12]

On the other hand, as is well known, this intelligentsia's opposition to the often described economic and social effects of
the British conquest was rationalized by Occidental slogans of
nationalism, though Buddhist organizations were used as means
of mass pressure on British power in the 1920's and 1930's. But
to the mind of the unwesternized rural masses, Buddhist goals
remained a primary aim of the struggle for independence from
the colonial system which had undermined Burma's economic
bases for her monastic institutions and thereby the bases for the
meditation which alone was to free men forever from the realm of
Impermanence and Suffering.

And the "Red Dragon" party song of the Thakin nationalist
revolutionaries of the later 1930's explicitly postulates as an aim
of the independence struggle the restoration or establishment of
Burma's prosperity "so that the poor will be enabled to build
monasteries,"[13] that is, economic reforms *as means* for the pursuit
of Nirvāṇa as the *goal*.

One of the key concepts of Burma's socialism is the idea of
Lokka Nibbān, a kind of earthly Nirvāṇa as designation for a
state of absolute harmony. Many anglicized Burmans believe the
notion of Lokka Nibbān to be of Marxist origin, a Marxist in-
novation in Burmese political terminology. But this term had
appeared in Thakin Kudaw Hmine's book *Thakin-Tīkā* in
1938.[14] And as Thakin Kudaw Hmine does not understand English, it cannot be the result of direct Western, including Marxist,
influences on him. On the other hand, the antisocialist, traditionalist Buddhist preacher U Nye Ya also demanded (perhaps
even earlier?) the kind of independence "that would establish a
Nirvāṇa in this world."[15] While I have not yet succeeded in
tracing the earliest use of this term, all evidence indicates that it
is not a pragmatic adaptation to Burma's postwar political requirements but rather is to be understood as an offshoot of cer-

tain secularizing trends in Burma's Buddhist thought of the
1920's: the concept of Lokka Hibbān echoes the activistic, "nationalistic" Buddhism of Sayadaw U Ottama, the leading "political monk" of the 1920's, whose monastic following already quite
explicitly emphasized the attainment of such political and social
conditions as are propitious for the quest towards Nirvāṇa.[16] And
as prototype for the selflessness of the liberation movement U
Ottama invoked the Bodhisattva ideal (of renouncing personal
liberation until the liberation of all beings from Suffering is
achieved),[17] just as in 1948 U Nu attributed to Aung San, the
murdered father of Burma's independence, Bodhisattva-like
qualities of selfless abnegation[18] (as have been found associated
with the ethos of Buddhist kingship).

Once the struggle for independence had been won, Burmese
statesmen like U Nu were no longer primarily concerned with an
Anglo-Saxon frame of reference to appeal to English audiences,
but were confronted by the nonwesternized majority of Burma's
people with its traditionalist outlook. This traditionalism has
affected the thought of the decisive revolutionary Thakin group
of the subsequent Anti-Fascist People's Freedom League through
such figures as its one-time president Thakin Thei Ku Daw Gyi,*
and particularly the ardent Buddhist U Ba Choe, a Burmese poet
and editor of the once influential journal *Di-do*, a close friend
of U Nu since his student days. U Ba Choe, a member of the
Burmese Cabinet who was murdered together with Aung San in
1947, was an outstanding specialist on Burmese folklore.

The folkloric tradition about primeval perfection with the
absence of the notion of Self and community of property was
interpreted by U Nu as an argument for socialism. Thus U Nu
declared in 1949 (and then again in 1950) that when the world
began, the material needs of all peoples were satisfied by nature
without effort, but that greed had moved them to appropriate
supplies beyond their immediate necessities and to separate them
as private property, and that this has caused want and misery
ever since. He emphasized that socialism is the teaching which
can bring humanity *back* to that blissful past.[19] Earlier, in 1948,

*Thakin Thei Ku Daw Gyi is a socialist descendant of King Mindon, who
married a daughter of Burma's last monarch, Thibaw (1879-1885).

he declared that property has only a functional place as means for the pursuit of Nirvāṇa (through meditation) and that the class struggle had arisen out of the illusion about the inherent value of property, that this illusion has caused bloodshed throughout history, so that its overcoming would usher in the Nirvāṇa in this world (Lokka Nibbān) through a perfect society.[20]

Thus U Nu's Buddhist socialism appears against the background of Burma's intellectual history not as purely pragmatic adaptation to postwar political requirements but as a modernized expression of ideas deep rooted in Burma's Buddhist heritage of the Aśokan tradition.[21] The economic and sociological environment of U Nu's political life has been regularly discussed by practically all American writers on postwar Burma and therefore need not be considered here. An intellectual biography of U Nu *in the context of* Burma's history of ideas indicates fewer pragmatic adaptations of ideology to circumstance than have appeared to those observers who cannot help taking pragmatism for granted. While his political shifts have been pragmatic enough, they have been mainly shifts in emphasis and in terminology. If they have been overestimated and the inherent consistency of U Nu's thought underestimated, it may be largely because his writings have never been collected and examined by historians in their totality. For example, his prewar essay "Kyan-daw buthama" (which U Nu told me was written in 1935) indicates that already at the beginning of his political career his image of capitalism referred to its underlying utilitarian primacy of the Self, the Self in which Buddhism sees the basic illusion and a cause of Suffering. Already in 1935 he blamed it for people's turning away from Buddhism, maintaining that not the elimination of capitalism, nor even the prosperity of the people, were ends in themselves, that only Buddhist goals were.[22]

Buddhist soteriology was—and has remained—primary in U Nu's thought, socialist economics secondary. As for the social ethos of medieval Burma, so for U Nu's ideology a welfare state (providing the economic presuppositions for meditation) is only a means, the overcoming of the Illusion of the Self—and release from the bonds of attachment to transitory existence—the final aim. Throughout U Nu's ideological adjustments between Buddhism, Fabianism, and Marxism, socialism and the welfare state have remained for him consistently economic means for Buddhist eschatological goals. Even when advocating Marxist unification, U Nu never accepted the Marxist *philosophy*. When in 1958 he formally rejected Marxism, he did not thereby completely reject Marxist *economics*. It is true that his more Marxist (revisionist) rivals like Kyaw Nyein of the Stable AFPFL (in 1959) also occasionally used some Buddhist slogans. But the latter explicitly explained to me that this was done after the pattern of Occidental socialism and Christian democratic parties and not out of Burmese tradition. This constituted a difference between the essentially (though no longer nominally) revisionist Marxist sources of the socialism of the Stable AFPFL faction and U Nu's more traditionalist outlook—in emphasis if not in content. And U Nu's traditionalist charisma is reflected both in folkloric identifications of his personality with the "Sedja Min," the expected ideal Burmese Buddhist ruler of the future and bearer of a social utopia,[23] and "enlightened" accusations that he is influenced by the example of medieval Burmese kings.

Precisely his closeness to the traditional Burmese folk outlook made U Nu suspect among the bureaucratic elite of English education and utilitarian outlook of the London School of Economics. Since the colonial period their social superiority has rested precisely on their enlightenment in British style and corresponding notions about the "backwardness" of the culturally more Burmese rural majority. For such successors of the British colonial administrators a statesman who takes folkloric (what they call "superstitious") notions of the "uneducated" villagers seriously—and even formulates his platform in their direction—committed "treason on the educated class." (Thus on July 6th, 1959, Dr. Hla Myint, then Rector of the University of Rangoon, declared in his official capacity to the writer that "Buddhism is unimportant for Burma politically" and that "Burma has no original ideas worth studying.") But all Buddhist abbots of the main monasteries of Sagaing, Ava, Amarapura, and Mandalay, the historical centers of Burmese culture, have (with one exception) told the writer that U Nu (who at the time of the interviews, in 1959, was out of power) came closest to the ideal Buddhist statesman in the tradition of Aśoka. In his elaborate election platform of November 16th, 1959, U Nu made reference to this Cakkavatī ideal of the perfect Buddhist ruler—a notion that inspired, for example, the above-quoted inscription of King Kyanzitthā in the 1090's—and described his Buddhist socialism, reiterating (as in 1935) that acquisition economy had developed out of the Illusion of the Self which Buddhism aims to overcome, and that it obstructs a social order that would make meditation economically possible for all, thereby permitting universal liberation from impermanence.[24]

Such ideas of U Nu have not been taken seriously by the culturally anglicized—like the editor of the *Nation*, a Rangoon newspaper in the English language that constitutes the bulk of the source material on which much Western writing on contemporary Burma is based. Such ideas of U Nu have not been taken seriously by area experts, who—in the tradition of Protestant missionary education—may concede to Burma a right to political independence but cannot easily grant the existence of a living Buddhist source of social ethics as alternative to Protestant utilitarian values. But if these concepts of U Nu have been lightly dismissed by such Burma experts, they have been taken very seriously indeed by the Burmese people themselves, whom they reminded of what have been long cherished ideals: U Nu was given an overwhelming majority in the elections of February 6th, 1960. His victory was a triumph of charismatic personality over a party machine, of Burmese tradition over imported slogans.[25]

NOTES

1. J. Cady, *A Modern History of Burma* (Ithaca, 1958).
2. J. R. Andrus, *Burmese Economic Life* (Stanford, 1948).
3. H. Tinker, *The Union of Burma: A Study of the First Years of Independence* (London, 1957).
4. G. McT. Kahin (ed.), *Government and Politics of Southeast Asia* (Ithaca, 1959).
5. The Shwegugyi Pagoda inscription translated from the Pāli by G. H. Luce. In: *Journal of the Burma Research Society*, X (1920), Part i, pp. 69-74.
6. Sarkisyanz, *Russland und der Messianismus des Orients (Tuebingen*, 1955), pp. 327-368.
7. Abridged from Kyanzitthā's Shwezigon Pagoda inscription, translation from Mōn in *Epigraphia Birmanica*, Vol. I, Part ii, edited by Ch. Duroiselle (Rangoon, 1920), pp. 117, 123, 142, 146, 166.
8. Seya U Po U, *Bodayaza Min Sedja* (Rangoon, 1955), pp. 140, 142, etc.; Zeyawadi Kyaung: Seyadaw (U Win), . . . *Budayaza Sedja Min la-pyi* (Mandalay, 1953), pp. 52, 54 ff.

9. Interview at a Mandalay pagoda (September 2, 1959) with astrologer who, because of political circumstances of that time, asked not to be identified by name.
10. *Manukyay Dhammathat* (Rangoon, 1953), pp. 3, 5.
11. Kudaw Hmine, *Thakin-Tīkā* (Rangoon, 1938), pp. 163 ff.
12. Sarkisyanz, "Thakin Kudaw Hmine, 'Burma's Rabindranath Tagore,'" unpublished Communication to the American Oriental Society, March 30, 1960.
13. Text of the Naga-ni Song as supplied by the Burmese Broadcasting Corporation, Rangoon.
14. Kudaw Hmine, *Thakin-Tīkā*, p. 181.
15. Nye Ya, *Lo-la ye alin* (Rangoon, 1952 reprint), pp. 13, 15; date of original publication not specified in reprint.
16. Zeyawadi U Thilasara, in *Pinnya Alin*, September 1, 1923.
17. Bhama-khit U Ba Yin, *Sayadaw U Ottama* (Amsterdam, 1959?), pp. 26 f.
18. U Nu's speech of April 16th, 1948: Thakin Nu, *Mein Khon-mya* (Rangoon, 1949), p. 42.
19. *Ibid.*, p. 108 (speech of July 19, 1950); Burma Ministry of Information. Thakin Nu, *Towards Peace and Democracy* (Rangoon, 1949), p. 129.
20. Tain: pyi pyu hlut-daw. *Myanma hnaingan-daw . . . (paliman) sahtama nyi-la khan hmat htam:*, Vol. VI, #30 (Rangoon, 1949), pp. 1179 ff. (U Nu's speech on October 11, 1948, delivered during the parliamentary debates on the Land Nationalization Act).
21. Sarkisyanz, *Russland und der Messianismus des Orients*, pp. 330-337, 350-361.
22. U Thein Pe Min (ed.), *Buwada hnin Dobama* (Rangoon, 1954), pp. 57, 61 ff, 66.
23. U Po U, *Bodayaza Min Sedja*, p. 142, as interpreted, for instance, by U Maung Gyi Daw Thein, the publisher of the corresponding prophecies in our interview of August 15, 1959.
24. *Bama-khit* (Rangoon) of November 17, 1959.
25. Sarkisyanz, "U Nu's Sieg: Der geistige Hintergrund der neuesten politischen Entwicklung in Burma," *Europa-Archiv*, XV (1960), No. 15, pp. 477-482.

The Changing Pattern of Religion and Politics in Burma

FRED R. VON DER MEHDEN
University of Wisconsin

The recent successful effort of Burmese politicians to use Buddhism to gain political support is but a contemporary manifestation of similar attempts made by Burmese leaders since the advent of British rule in the nineteenth century. Developed by the early nationalists, this technique has been employed by the entire spectrum of Burmese politicians from monarchist to communist. The role of religion in politics has, however, undergone a transition from being a controlling and governing force to its present status as a propaganda tool which may set the tone to politics but very rarely governs it. This paper attempts to analyze the changing pattern of Buddhism in politics in Burma.

I

Foreign observers have often commented on the fact that the *pongyi* (Buddhist monk) in Burma differs from his counterpart in neighboring Thailand in that he actively participates in politics. Yet today's monk is but a shadow of his old political self. During the high tide of *pongyi* activity in the nationalist movement in the 1920's the *sangha* (monkhood) influenced political life on both an individual and a collective basis. Monks were to be found as members of the executive boards of nationalist parties, on the managerial staff of newspapers, as political speakers, and generally in the forefront of the nationalist movement. The *pongyis* also formed organizations such as the General Council of Sangha Associations which were influential among all sections of the nationalists during the 1920's. As a group *pongyis* often screened candidates for office, once audited the funds of the

major nationalist party, and, after that party split, controlled its
most radical splinter. As one former *pongyi* politician described
the situation in the early twenties, "all was yellow" (the traditional color of monks' robes).

This power had waned by the beginning of World War II
under the impact of reactions to excesses by *pongyi* nationalists,
an increasing sophistication among lay politicians, and a return
to religious values within the *sangha*. The final blow to mass
political activity of the monks was the advent to power of the
Marxist-minded, secularly oriented leadership of the Anti-Fascist
People's Freedom League (AFPFL). Led by Aung San, a man
suspicious of *pongyi* political ambitions, and containing a number of young university graduates, this group sought to contain
sangha activity in the religious realm. Even U Nu, a man of un-
doubted Buddhist sympathies, wrote bitterly of *pongyi* wartime
efforts to influence government policy.[1] These reactions were
partly ideological and partially due to memories of the use of
pongyis by their old political rivals.

Thus when the AFPFL came into undisputed power at the
end of the war, the *sangha* found itself with less political power
than it had held during the colonial period. Instead of their being accepted as a controlling element in the nationalist movement, the immediate postwar attitude was that the religious were
to remain outside of politics. In line with the recommendations
of the older apolitical *pongyis* who had withdrawn from politics
during the 1930's (but in opposition to the traditionally more
politically oriented Young Sangha Associations), all monks were
constitutionally prohibited from voting or standing for parliamentary elections.[2] The *sangha* was also cautioned by AFPFL
leaders to partake only in religious duties and to eschew religious
intolerance. Aung San denounced the previous political activities of the *sangha* and what he termed the confusion and quarrels
of "priestcraft" (which he differentiated from priesthood).[3]

The first years of the AFPFL were the nadir of *pongyi* political influence, but subsequent years have not brought a return to
the prewar situation. Efforts during the first decade of AFPFL
rule to achieve *pongyi* aspirations such as support for monastery
schools and the establishment of a Buddhist state were abortive.
Nor did three laws which Nu introduced in 1950 to reform the

sangha meet with universal *pongyi* approval. The objections to the bills, which established ecclesiastical courts, founded a Pali university, and formed a national *pongyi* organization, were based upon criticisms of government interference with religion as well as upon disappointment at not being chosen to sit on various boards and organizations.[4] One case in which the *sangha* did sway the government was in the field of religious instruction. In 1954, according to U Nu, certain *sayadaws* (abbots) called upon him to meet the threat of Communism by means of Buddhist instruction in the schools. He agreed, but also advanced the idea of Moslem and Christian instruction in their schools. Three monks from Mandalay objected, so he changed his mind and withdrew all religious teaching. Again the monks objected, so he reinstated only Buddhist instruction.[5] This was a rare case, for in the legislative field the *sangha* has generally been unsuccessful or disinterested.

This does not mean that the monks are without political power in contemporary Burma. It is true that they cannot vote and as a group have little interest in national policy, but the respect which the *pongyi* receives in the village allows him to influence the villagers in areas outside of religion if he so desires. The extent to which the monk can influence political events varies, with his greatest strength in rural areas in general and upper Burma proper in particular. In the villages this impact is more on a personal level, whereas in the cities *pongyis* often attempt to operate on a group basis. Generally, these individuals and groups refrain from political activities, but when a religious issue is before the country and during elections they are apt to appear upon the scene. For example, during the 1959 municipal elections, one newspaper found it noteworthy to report that in one municipality *pongyis* had *not* been active. Although the *sangha* as a whole remained neutral during the 1960 elections, various *sangha* organizations supported the party of their choice through speeches, statements, published propaganda, and the more subtle method of a word-of-mouth campaign. It should be observed that these monks rarely explain their advocacy of various candidates on any basis other than religion. Traditionally, their candidate is characterized as one who can best defend Buddhism or support particular religious issues which the *pongyis* advocate. The voter is at times confused by having different *sang-ha* organizations supporting opposing candidates on similar grounds.

In their efforts to gain votes by displaying their religious ardor, the candidates continually publicize acts of obeisance to the *sangha*. Parties and nominees provide food and robes for *pongyis*, announce that *sayadaws* have been approached for advice, and attempt to gain the backing of the *sangha* organizations. It is, however, no longer considered proper to follow the prewar practice of touring one's constituency with *pongyi* supporters. The urban population now reacts somewhat cynically to the political use of *pongyis*, but in spite of this it remains a politically effective weapon. The pattern differs most markedly from that of the prewar period in that the politically conscious monks no longer determine policy and now often find themselves the pawns of politicians.

II

The diminishing role of religious personnel in politics may partially be explained by the diluted content of religion in the national ideology. Members of older prewar parties such as the General Council of Burmese Associations found it impossible to define national goals without including Buddhism. A major reason for desiring freedom from the British was to eliminate foreign religious control and establish a state in which Buddhism could prosper and political life would be based upon Buddhist principles. According to one prewar nationalist newspaper, "Without being free from bondage . . . one can hardly find peace in one's heart or in one's environment in which the Buddhist way of life may be practiced . . . ."[6] Older *pongyi* politicians whom the author has interviewed stated to a man that they entered into nationalist activities to preserve and protect Buddhism, and their views were repeated by a number of politicians who described the religious issue as a vital factor in the nationalist ideology.

Buddhism remains an essential ingredient in the Burmese way of life, but the leaders who articulate the nationalist ideology no longer emphasize it as did their predecessors. Two exceptions have been U Nu, who continually expresses himself in Buddhist terms, and more recently the army, which has used religion to develop national unity against the Communists.[7] Even these two exceptions must be regarded with care. Nu, although he is apparently sincere in his religious leanings, has displayed marked caution in allowing the *sangha* any influence in the decision-making processes of his government. The army, on the other hand, used religion as a manipulative device against the Communist movement in what recent evidence has shown to be only a short-lived experiment. Other leaders such as Kyaw Nyein, U Ba Swe, U Tin, and most of the men who came into power with the AFPFL have reflected more Aung San's secularist leanings. These men were not anti-Buddhist, but did tend to be somewhat anticlerical and in favor of the separation of church and state. Describing the Thakin group from which most of the younger leaders came, Aung San boasted, "In fact, it is the only non-racial, non-religious and impersonal movement that has ever existed in Burma. Formerly and still now among a certain section of the Burmese public, nationalism was conceived in terms of race and religion."[8]

This attitude led the early AFPFL to emphasize equality and freedom for all religions, and party statements usually neglected any mention of the Buddhist faith. For example, the original AFPFL Manifesto of 1944 declared, "Freedom of conscience should be established. The State should remain neutral on religious questions."[9] When the Constitution was formulated, this position was firmly supported by Aung San when he argued against Deedok U Ba Cho's positions that independence would be empty without a Buddhist state religion. To this Aung San replied that Burma was a secular state. Among the young AFPFL leaders religion just did not have a part to play in defining national goals and was rarely discussed at party conferences.

In the years since independence, many politicians have toned down their secularist statements as they have found them politically unwise. It is interesting to see men such as Kyaw Nyein, Ba Swe, and even Nu compromise with their previous positions under the exigencies of political life, for there can be little doubt that the successful politician must play to the people's belief that the state has a duty (possibly its only duty in their minds) to foster and protect Buddhism. This U Nu masterfully developed during the postwar period and particularly during the 1960 elections. At the same time, there is a certain tolerance toward other religions, a degree of anticlericalism, and an interest in form rather than content which was not so prevalent in the prewar nationalist movement.

III

A further aspect of this changing pattern revolves around the question of the role which religion is to play in the state. Again, early nationalists hoped that following independence Buddhism and its clergy would be returned to the place it was conceived to have held prior to the British conquest. During the period of the Burmese monarchy there existed a state religion which helped to set the character of the government, and the monks intermittently influenced state politics. Upon the final victory of the British in 1885, direct religious influence on the governmental apparatus ceased with the nonrecognition of Buddhism as the state religion, deterioration of the *sangha's* role in education, and elimination of the formal place of the monk in the councils of state. Those religious nationalists who hoped to see Buddhism as an integral part of the state after independence were disappointed. Although Buddhism was constitutionally recognized as having a "special position" as the majority religion of the Burmese, there was no official acceptance of Buddhism as the state religion.[10]

Instead, Burma found herself in the somewhat anomalous position of having no state religion but with a prime minister who on the one hand preached religious equality, and on the other granted special favors to the Buddhist faith. For example, U Nu agreed to have Buddhism taught in state schools, once declared that only a Buddhist could become President (upon which the Constitution is silent and his colleagues ambiguous) and got Parliament to grant six million kyat (approximately $1,250,000) to build the grandiose Peace Pagoda, artificial cave, and surrounding Buddhist University for the Sixth World Buddhist Synod. Critics of the latter claimed that Indian traders received import licenses for aiding the building fund and that the whole project was a useless expense to a country vitally in need of money for social improvements.[11] Finally, there have been allegations that U Nu has often accepted the advice of religious leaders in opposition to members of his cabinet. For example, U Tun Pe resigned from his position as Minister of Union Culture on the basis (among other reasons) that religious elements were interfering with government decisions. There is no question that Nu's personal interest in Buddhism helped to set a religious tone for his administrations.

If Burma under Nu can be described as sympathetic toward Buddhism, it can also be characterized by its interest in the outward forms of religion rather than by the direct influence of Buddhism on the decision-making process. An interesting example of this situation has developed in the religious state issue. When I left Burma in April 1960, few of those proposing a Buddhist state considered that its adoption would presage any real change in the structure of processes of government. In a revealing statement the Organisation to Establish Buddhism as a State Religion answered a series of questions on the impact of a state religion on Burma and its people. Among other points, it declared that 1) no religion would suffer, 2) the principle of aiding other religions would continue, 3) the question of the necessity of having the President and ministers Buddhist would be decided in accordance with the Constitution and democracy, 4) the *sangha* would not run for seats in Parliament, 5) Buddhist citizens would be expected to live by the principles of Buddhism and other religions according to their own tenets, 6) Buddhism would be compulsory for Buddhist students, and 7) the establishment of a Buddhist state was not against socialism, science, or good international relations.[12] In other words, no change other than form was contemplated.

IV

Possibly the best contemporary example of the impact of religion on politics was the 1960 parliamentary election.[13] Paradoxically, although religion was a key element in the victory of U Nu and his Clean faction of the AFPFL, it was not officially recognized as an issue in the campaign. This can be partially explained by the feeling that religion and politics should not be mixed, but a more important factor was the Constitutional prohibition of "the abuse of religion for political purposes." Officially interpreted, this meant religion must be kept out of the campaign. In fact, it displayed the devious means by which religion is injected into postwar Burmese politics.

The major protagonists in the battle were the Clean AFPFL under U Nu and the Stable AFPFL under U Ba Swe and U Kyaw Nyein. These men had been part of the united AFPFL until that party had split in 1958. The army caretaker government which ruled for sixteen months following the deterioration of civilian politics allowed completely free elections in February 1960 in order that the politicians might again rule the country. This started the electoral battle in which religion was an important weapon. The opening salvo came from the Clean camp prior to the official start of the campaign when U Nu promised a Buddhist state if elected. Having reiterated a promise that he had previously made but never kept, and after having pointed out that his statement was before the campaign and therefore not unconstitutional, Nu entered a monastery for six weeks.

The Clean position immediately put the Stable forces on the defensive. At first the idea of a state religion was attacked as a violation of the united AFPFL's previous stand that a Buddhist state would divide multireligious Burma. It was further declared that Nu was extremely vague in describing the value of such a situation, only promising that it would in no way endanger other religions. Of what good then was a Buddhist state, his enemies asked. Finally, the action of the Clean leader was described as an unconstitutional use of religion for political purposes. However, the Stable faction soon discovered that the Clean tactic was winning favor in upper Burma and among the women voters, and in mid-December the Swe-Nyein faction succumbed to the religious issue. In fact, it came out with an eleven-point program which promised more specific aids to Buddhism than had its opponents.

The Stable forces were working under a number of handicaps. On the religious state issue, as in others during the campaign, they moved too slowly and too cautiously. The co-heads of the party, Ba Swe and Kyaw Nyein, had never publicized their devotion to Buddhism as had Nu, and in fact both were rumored to be rather indifferent toward religion. During the campaign the Stable leaders attempted to change this image of themselves by giving food and gifts to *pongyis,* and Ba Swe followed Nu into a monastery. These acts were almost futile, for their opponent is the symbol of Buddhism to large numbers of his countrymen. It was Nu who convened the Sixth World Buddhist Synod, a feat which only monarchs had previously accomplished. It was Nu who had for years sprinkled his speeches with Buddhist stories and sayings. It was Nu who was looked upon by many people as a Buddha in the becoming. (Some of his opponents called upon the people to help him become a Buddha by depriving him of office so that he could spend full time at the job.)

During the weeks prior to the election, the religious issue was in a curious never-never land in which the man who initiated it denied that it was an issue, while his colleagues praised his devoutness and his critics attempted to diminish the public character which he had built over the years. The Stable charged Nu with being an opportunist and called the Buddhist yellow color on the Clean ballot boxes a trick to fool the people. None of these efforts appears to have been overly effective. The picture of Nu as a devout defender of the faith had been too long in the making, and attacks upon him had a tendency to backfire.

The Clean and Stable were not the only forces interested in the battle. The deputy prime minister, U Lun Baw, speaking for the electoral watchdog Ne Win government, warned against using religion for political ends and warned the monks to confine themselves to Buddhism. The monks on their part maintained a tenuous neutrality, although obviously pleased that both parties were so vigorously defending the faith. Some *sangha* organizations in Rangoon and Mandalay did take the traditional path of party affiliation. The monks in Mandalay were largely pro-Clean, but only a minority joined pro-Nu political *sangha* associations. In Rangoon, the Union Sangha League, another small pro-Clean organization, applauded Nu's position on a Buddhist state and called the Stable fascist. The Stable also had its *sangha* groups in Mandalay and Rangoon, which were active in both the municipal and parliamentary elections.

Neither the charges of the opposition nor the warnings of the constitutionalists could change the Nu tide. There were, of course, other powerful forces behind the Clean victory, including Nu's popularity, poor strategy on the part of the Stable party, and the dislike for the army rule which was linked to the Stable.

At the same time, it is impossible to deny the religious flavor of the campaign which could only aid U Nu and his party.

It can be argued that this election marked a return to the pre-war pattern of religious politics. If so, it was more reminiscent of the late thirties when politicians used religion and the religious as tools. It was not a parallel situation to the twenties when the Buddhist clergy acted as a powerful decision-making force within the nationalist movement. Most observers agree that Nu has successfully used the religious issue to gain an important electoral victory, but few expect that this will mean a significant resurgence of *pongyi* political power or that the state, even if it is a Buddhist state, will have its policies much more defined by Buddhist principles than are the United States' policies by Christian principles.

In conclusion, Burma remains a Buddhist nation, proud of its religious heritage, and the government, at least under Nu, is sympathetic toward the idea of fostering the faith. Surface manifestations of governmental interest in Buddhism can be seen in obeisance to monks, the import of holy relicts, speeches and pilgrimages by political leaders. At the same time, the direct influence of Buddhism and its clergy on the daily operations of the state and the actions of most politicians appears minimal. This diminished strength of religious influence is in striking contrast to the high tide of prewar *pongyi* power when the clergy was a vital political force. Even if Nu stands by his promise for a Buddhist state, the consensus is that its advent will not re-establish the old order.

NOTES

1. Thakin Nu, *Burma under the Japanese* (London: Macmillan, 1954), p. 91.
2. Constitution of the Union of Burma, Section II, and Parliamentary Elections Act, 1948.
3. Aung San, *Burma's Challenge*, mimeographed, n.d.
4. John Cady, *A History of Burma* (Ithaca: Cornell University Press, 1958), pp. 611-612.
5. This is Nu's version given in reply to critics during the 1959-60 election campaign. *Nation*, November 24, 1959.
6. *The Knowledge*, September 1, 1923 (translated by the author from the Burmese).
7. See Fred R. von der Mehden, "Burma's Religious Campaign against Communism," *Pacific Affairs*, xxxiii: 3 (August, 1960).
8. *New Burma*, May 10, 1940.

9. *The New Burma* (Rangoon: Nay Win Kyi Press, n.d.).
10. See Maung Maung, *Burma's Constitution* (The Hague: Nijhoff, 1959), pp. 98-99.
11. See U Tun Pe, *Why I Resigned from the Cabinet; Statement before Press Conference on August 13, 1953*, Rangoon, 1953.
12. *The Burman,* March 7, 1960.
13. See R. Butwell and F. von der Mehden, "The 1960 Election in Burma," *Pacific Affairs,* xxxiii: 2 (June, 1960).

Civilians and Soldiers in Burma

RICHARD BUTWELL

University of Illinois

The relinquishment of high political office by Burma's General Ne Win in April, 1960 has generally been regarded as unique among the experiences of the several newly independent lands in which power has been seized by the military. A soldier administration which had replaced the government of Premier U Nu eighteen months earlier turned over the reins of state to this very same Nu. In doing so, it clearly gave the civilian politicians a second chance to try their hand at giving Burma effective government.

Throughout most of the first decade of Burma's regained independence, the Army generally acquiesced in most of the non-military decisions made by the politicians, partly because it was preoccupied with fighting various kinds of insurrectionists, but in part also because its leadership and the leading political figures were old revolutionary comrades who liked and trusted one another.

The bonds, however, began to wear thin towards the end of the first decade of self-rule, as various of the lesser figures of the preindependence period began to assume greater political importance. Colonel Maung Maung, number three man in the Ne Win administration, put it this way: "When the Second World War was over and we had obtained our independence, the cream of the resistance movement stayed with the Burma Army, and most of the rest became politicians. It was irksome to find that those who could not hold their own in the Army came in time to be our political superiors."[1]

Colonel Maung Maung did not mean, of course, such leaders as Nu, Ba Swe, and Kyaw Nyein, but he apparently did mean the several "Bo"'s, or "captains," of the resistance years against the Japanese who came to occupy positions of importance in the pre-

Ne Win government: Bo Min Gaung, Bo Hmu Aung, and others.

The background of Burma's top Army leadership, while similar to that of the civilian politicians, contrasts markedly with the bulk of the officer group. Recruitment in recent years has been mainly from the ranks of the college graduates, and there is an ever-larger body of officers who represent professional soldiers who never were political agitators. It is within the ranks of these men that there has probably been the greatest amount of dissatisfaction with the results of rule by the civilian politicians.

The role of the Army in Burmese life, almost from the start of the postindependence period, has been more than the maintenance of external defense or of internal security. The Army as a group has been called upon consistently to perform various nonmilitary functions. Many of the highest decisions of state, moreover, were cleared with the top military leadership, including all of Premier Nu's various overtures to the Communists (and other rebels) to end their fight against the government.[2]

There is considerable evidence that General Ne Win had serious doubts about the wisdom of too heavy involvement on the Army's part in nonmilitary functions, however. On several occasions he called for continued recognition of the principle of civilian supremacy in Burmese government, and he also cautioned the military against taking sides in the struggle for power among contending political groups. On the whole, their Commander-in-Chief's words were heeded by the military until the summer of 1958.

In the previous spring the party that had regained independence for the country, the Anti-Fascist People's Freedom League, split into two approximately equal factions.[3] One was headed by Premier Nu, the other by U Ba Swe and U Kyaw Nyein, who were major figures in the government in the first decade of independence. Nu's faction called itself the "Clean" A.F.P.F.L., the Swe-Nyein group the "Stable" A.F.P.F.L. In a parliamentary vote of confidence the "Clean" won by a narrow margin, saved from defeat by the votes of the Communist-oriented National Unity Front.

This Communist backing in the showdown vote cost Nu some prestige in the Army, not because he was regarded as pro-Communist, but because of fears that the Communists would exploit the situation Nu helped to create by not rejecting their support. The tougher attitude assumed by the Communist rebels subsequent to the A.F.P.F.L. split also caused Army misgivings about Nu. It was the feeling of the Army leadership that Nu, by bringing the split into the open, gave the Communists renewed hopes of victory through exploitation of the differences among the anti-Communist politicians.

The fears of the military leadership mounted in early September when the Army was explicitly labeled public enemy number one at a "Clean" A.F.P.F.L. rally held in the compound of Premier Nu.[4] Nu disclaimed any knowledge of the charges, made within hearing distance of his working office in the Prime Minister's official residence. But the damage had already been done. Either Nu knew that the charges would be made, or he was not in control of his party (which actually was the case).

The rest of September saw the situation go from bad to worse. A political war—in a literal sense—seemed to be shaping up between the "Clean" and "Stable" factions. Attention of the Nu government was called to large collections of arms known to be in existence in various areas of lower Burma, but the government did not authorize the military to bring these in. Clandestine movement of certain units of the Union Military Police (under "Clean" Minister of Interior Bo Min Gaung) caused the Army leadership to question the purpose behind such action. The factionalism afflicting the politicians also seemed to be spreading to the Army. Moreover, rumors were circulating of a plot to assassinate the top Army leaders. It was in these circumstances that the Army moved to depose Premier Nu.[5]

The Army seizure of power was motivated primarily by two considerations: the steadily deteriorating state of law and order, and the fact that the Army was now the object of attack by some of the non-Communists as well as the Communists.

General Ne Win, however, was a reluctant candidate for the premiership. Content with the power and status of Army commander-in-chief and lacking political ambition, he had to be convinced. This was done by Colonels Aung Gyi and Maung Maung, principal figures on the Army side of the takeover, who realized that they could never move without Ne Win. A virtual ultimatum, accordingly, was given Nu to step down. Nu, however, came up with a face-saving formula by which he was to resign and ask Ne Win to form a caretaker government to rule for six months and restore law and order before free elections were held. The Army leaders, conscious of the benefits of constitutional procedure, agreed.

From the start it was clear that Premier General Ne Win's was to be more than a caretaker regime. Not only did the General's government move vigorously to restore law and order, but it also made and sought to implement decisions that significantly changed the country's basic economic policies. Greater emphasis was placed on increasing agricultural production and less on industrial development, while a larger role was allocated to private enterprise in various phases of the economy, including the international marketing of rice, Burma's number one export commodity. Politically, the Ne Win government inaugurated a country-wide movement called the National Solidarity Associations for the purpose of inculcating the values of law and order and serving as a check against possible future excesses on the part of the politicians.[6]

U Nu, who had been saved from inglorious ouster from office by the constitutional formula he had devised, regarded the Army's multisided activity as a breach of faith with him. When General Ne Win indicated at the end of six months that it was not yet possible to hold free elections because the country was still disturbed, Nu apparently felt tricked.

Since it regarded Ba Swe and the "Stable" party as a lesser evil, moreover, the Ne Win government clearly favored Nu's opponents. Large numbers of Nu's supporters were arrested (many of them probably for valid reasons), but the attack on followers of Ba Swe and Kyaw Nyein was mild in comparison. An effort was also made to link the "Clean" faction with both the above-ground Communist National Unity Front and the Communist insurgents. Forced by circumstances but also aware of the political benefits involved, U Nu accordingly took to attacking the caretaker regime, being the only person brave enough to do so directly and consistently during the period of Army rule.[7]

Although the Army favored the "Stable" over the "Clean" party, its real preference was the election of a sufficiently large number of independents to hold the balance in parliament be-

tween the two factions of the A.F.P.F.L. One of the main un-
declared aims of the National Solidarity Association movement
was to encourage independents to run for parliament, and representatives of the Army sought to generate popular support for
them. Army leaders apparently hoped that such a body of independents, professional men of the sort who served the caretaker regime in various capacities, could be used to influence the
results of the legislative process. It was at a time when the military apparently still harbored such expectations that the government announced the holding of elections for the lower house, the
Chamber of Deputies.

There are several reasons for the Army's permitting the return of the civilians to office. The most important of these probably was the fact that the Ne Win government had fulfilled the
main requirement of its caretaker stewardship: the restoration of
law and order. There was, in short, no longer the threat to the
nation or the Army that had existed in 1958.

Secondly, the Army probably felt in September, 1959, when it
announced elections would be held, that it was not in fact turning power back to the same politicians functioning under the
same circumstances. U Nu's political stock was at an all-time low
at the time of the election announcement, and those who expected that he would again be Burma's premier formed a distinct
minority.

Thirdly, Burma's military leaders were clearly aware of the
mounting hostility of the populace towards the Army as a consequence of the haste of its reformism and its frequently arbitrary
behavior. Ne Win and his colleagues apparently reasoned that
an unpopular Army government would serve only the interests
of the Communists.

Fourthly, the personality of Ne Win himself was a factor in
the Army's departure from office. The frequently offered char-
acterization of Ne Win as lazy and lacking in ambition is an
oversimplification and is neither accurate nor fair. The General,
more than any other single person, is responsible for the development of the Burmese Army from practically nothing at the height
of the insurrections in 1949 to its present status as a highly regarded fighting force and a major factor in keeping independent
Burma's national head above water. Ne Win does not possess the

ambition to be prime minister, however. No doubt he was advised by some of his associates to hold off on the return of the civilians to office, but his power and prestige were such that, failing to gain his support, they were forced to go along with him.

Finally, once the decision to allow the civilians to return was made, there was no turning back. The sweep of the municipal elections by U Nu's "Clean" party in late 1959 left no doubt as to the popularity of the former Premier or the lack of popularity of the Army government.

The political situation in Burma following the February, 1960 election and the April return to office of U Nu on the wave of a tremendous expression of the voters' confidence differs considerably from that of the precaretaker period. It is now known that the Army is both willing and able to move against the politicians when it and the country are threatened. The Army also has shown itself capable of giving the nation better government than the politicians in the sense of a government that does things and does them well.[8] Nu, on the other hand, has returned to power on his own in the face of Army opposition (which was never explicitly stated as such).[9] In such a situation, what kind of relationship between soldiers and civilians in Burma may be expected in the immediate future?

It is the writer's opinion that U Nu is both sufficiently pleased with the fact of his comeback and possessed of such a desire to avoid conflict, largely for reasons of his particular kind of personality, that he will tend to forget past differences with the Army. He also is intelligent enough to know that he is on trial with the military leadership and will seek to avoid provoking the Army again. The Army, on the other hand, will give Nu and his colleagues a decent trial; they have to in view of public opinion, and Nu knows this.

The main reason why Nu must get along with the military is the fact that Burma's Army is unquestionably the single most important group in the life of his country today. The most obvious aspect of the Army's strength is its preponderant share of the country's military or police force. More than a hundred thousand strong, it is over twice the size of the national police (the present numbers of which exaggerate actual strength in view of the recent incorporation of the undisciplined Special Police

Reserves, which more than doubled the amount of police personnel).[10] Burma's national police is not on the model of the second army maintained formerly by Police Director-General Phao Sriyanon in neighboring Thailand and which was a factor for a while counterbalancing the strength and ambitions of then Army leader Sarit Thanarat. No Burmese government in the foreseeable future could maintain itself without the Army as a check against resurgence of large-scale terrorist activity, and no Burmese government could remain in power if the Army really wanted to topple it.

The Army, however, also is an economic power. Through its Defense Services Institute, it has come to be a major importer of a vast variety of goods ranging from coal to automobiles; it also operates the country's biggest department store, catches and sells fish, and runs a bookstore, restaurants, a bus line, the country's largest automobile service station, and a shoe factory. It is also in the banking, shipping, and construction businesses.[11] It has a major influence on private investment too, through its policy of selling out its various holdings after they have been put on an efficient operating basis.[12]

Although none of its officers ran for election in the February, 1960 elections, the Army has by no means gotten completely out of politics. The leadership of the Central Council of the National Solidarity Association movement remains in Army hands,[13] although these leaders have changed their minds as to the role the N.S.A.'s should play in national life. Their original intention[14] was that the N.S.A.'s should be a mass movement guarding against a return of the bullying excesses of some of the politicians in the precaretaker period, but the mass membership has lost interest in the N.S.A.'s since the return of U Nu to office. The belief that many persons joined the movement during the caretaker era because they felt it expedient to do so appears to be substantiated. The Army leadership now apparently regards the N.S.A. movement as elitist rather than mass and as an educational rather than as an action organization. Although the second role may differ from the Army's anticipations, it is still a political one.

In addition to its military, economic, and political resources, the Army also has a certain strength deriving from the quality of its personnel, who are generally more highly educated than the politicians and possess greater knowledge and dedication than the civil service. This has resulted in the Army's being called upon to perform various duties that might ordinarily be expected of the civilian administration or political appointees. Some of these duties are of major importance to Burma today. Army Colonel Saw Myint, for example, is head of the Frontier Areas Administration which directly rules large areas of crucial border territory.[15] It is the Army, too, that has been given the very important function of leading in the settlement of vast areas of the country with limited population. Army personnel and their families are sent to Israel to learn the ways of communal life and then return to Burma to help the government settle the more sparsely populated and underdeveloped parts of the country.[16]

The Army, in short, is today a much stronger force than it was before the 1958 takeover in terms of economic power, political activity, governmental experience, and probable backing from the small but influential educated Rangoon professional class.

Government in Burma since General Ne Win gave up office has deteriorated, however. Prices are once again soaring, garbage goes uncollected, and the administration appears to have slipped back into its old ways of perpetual buck-passing. Premier Nu, in his dealings with the student leaders demanding a reversal of the caretaker government's educational reforms, has shown himself only too willing to give in even to the pressures of undisciplined youth. The creation of various new advisory commissions gives evidence of a worsening of the problem of locating responsibility within the governmental system. There is every indication that day-to-day government in Burma will drop at least part of the way back to the old standards of inefficiency and possible corruption.

Does this mean the Army will seek to return to high political office? Probably not. General Ne Win and his colleagues put up with a great deal of inefficiency and corruption without intervention in the past, and they did not move when they did because of these considerations. The ever-changing personnel complexion of the Army, however, raises doubts as to how long the present leadership will be representative of the thought of the second-liners in this regard. There is a certain friendly tolerance of the shortcomings of the politicians on the part of Ne Win, stemming from the old days, but a new generation of professional soldiers is emerging and their answer a few years hence (or even sooner) may be very different from that of the soldier-premier who stepped down from office.

A serious deterioration of law and order, however—renewed attacks on the Army or efforts by the politicians to reduce the power of the Army—would probably bring an even quicker response from the military leadership than the events of September, 1958.

This U Nu presumably realizes. Yet Nu has not always been master in his own house, as witnessed by the Army-baiting "Clean" convention in the Prime Minister's own compound in September, 1958. Moreover, Nu has shown himself to be a man susceptible to flattery and the provocation of intense suspicion by those interested in using him for their own ends, as illustrated by the way Thakins Tin and Kyaw Dun convinced him that Ba Swe and Kyaw Nyein were plotting to kick him upstairs to the presidency in 1957. Ne Win was in attendance at the meeting at which this proposal was advanced (by Burma's Ambassador to Peiping, who wanted Nu to be a sort of Burmese Mao Tse-tung), and it is possible that this incident, for example, could be used again to stir up resentment on Nu's part—this time against his Army's chief. After all, the Army did throw Nu out of power.

Nu based a good part of his comeback campaign on the necessity to restore and further develop democracy in Burma.[17] There is no reason to question the sincerity of his intentions in this respect. The top Army leadership, moreover, gives evidence of ideological attraction to democracy,[18] if the politicians seriously endeavor to make it work. The trouble is that, aside from Nu and a few other politicians and a handful of intellectuals (including important members of the press), there seems to be limited support in the country for democratic government. Most of Nu's chief political lieutenants today are holdovers from the precaretaker period, and few of them can be realistically described as knowing what democracy is all about. The same can be said about most of those in the camp of the opposition "Stable" A.F.P.F.L.

Ironically, not only would Nu like the Army to have the kind of subordinate role it has in Western democracies, but Ne Win also apparently would like this. Others of the military leadership, however, appear to view the Army more as a vehicle of social and economic change which probably can not be carried out without a large or even exclusive share in political decision-making. The frequently displayed political adroitness of Premier Nu provides hope that he can adequately satisfy the aspirations of the Army in this respect. However, Nu's increasingly traditionalist outlook would seem to suggest a possible problem in intra-elite communications in the future, perhaps the near future, and this could have direct bearing on how long the younger Army modernists tolerate their Premier. In recent years the Army and Nu (and many of the other politicians, too) seem to have been moving in different directions intellectually.[19] Socialism continues to move the civilian politicians (as well as the Army leadership), but the pragmatic Army leaders have already given evidence that they understand better what Socialism is—and is not—than most of the sloganeering politicians. Unless the politicians move closer to the values and attitudes of the world beyond Burma, it is possible that it will matter little whether U Nu is a democrat or not.

The rise to power of Burma's Army in 1958 has its point of similarity—and dissimilarity—with the experiences of other undeveloped nations. The Burmese Army came to power when it appeared to have no alternative in terms of its own or the nation's survival (as it saw the situation). Presumably other armies would do the same, which makes the Burmese action quite typical. But it also seems that this was not the primary reason why Nasser or Kassem or Ayub Khan came to power at the time they did in the way they did—which makes the Burmese situation atypical. Ne Win seems never to have regarded himself as a kind of national messiah as Nasser, Kassem, or even Ayub Khan has. It is very possible, of course, that an Egyptian-Iraqi-Pakistani type of military takeover might have come in time in view of the forces building up in Burma, particularly within the military. The Army, however, was forced to seize power before disappointment and resentment with civilian failings had produced the same degree of response from within the Army ranks. This could have the effect of reducing the possibility of the Army's intervening again, and it could be an indirect boost to democracy's prospects in Burma.

Because Burma's Army leaders seized political power for the purpose of restoring law and order to save the nation and themselves, theirs would appear to be a rather unique experience. Honest and politically nonambitious, Burma's present military leaders gave up high office when they had fulfilled their mission. It would probably be in vain that those who would understand the next step in Pakistan, Iraq, or the United Arab Republic would look to Burma for suggestions. Indeed, it might well be that both the soldiers and civilians in Burma could look to these countries in anticipation of what still might be their fate in the years to come.

NOTES

1. This statement was made in an interview with the author, April 19, 1960.
2. Various senior officers so stated in conversations with the author in Rangoon in 1959-60.
3. See Frank N. Trager, "The Political Split in Burma," *Far Eastern Survey*, October, 1958, pp. 145-155, and J. S. Furnivall, *The Governance of Modern Burma* (New York: Institute of Pacific Relations, 1958), pp. 109-129.
4. U Sein Win, *The Split Story* (Rangoon: The Guardian, Ltd., 1959), p. 75.
5. Nu, of course, does not admit that this is the way things happened—nor do the top Army leaders, who also have an interest in not being publicly depicted as having seized power. Lesser politicians and officers are more frank, however, and their stories check out. For Nu's analysis of the developing situation that produced the change of governments, see "Speech delivered by the Hon'ble U Nu, Prime Minister, to the Conference of Union Youths on October 19," *Burma Weekly Bulletin*, October 23, 1958.
6. See the remarks of Vice Chief of Staff (Navy) Commodore Than Pe before the first conference of the Rangoon Divisional Council of the N.S.A. *The Nation*, November 30, 1959. The accomplishments of the Ne Win government are officially described in *The Nine Months After the Ten Years* (Rangoon: Ministry of Information, 1959) and *Is Trust Vindicated?* (Rangoon: Director of Information, 1960).
7. *The Government of the People* (Rangoon: "Clean" A.F.P.F.L., 1959) is an excellent illustration of U Nu's courageous outspokenness during this period. See also his *Stages of the Battle Against Oppression* (in Burmese) (Rangoon: "Clean" A.F.P.F.L., 1959) and *We Must Defend Democracy* (Rangoon: "Clean" A.F.P.F.L., 1959).
8. For the caretaker administration's own assessment of its record, see *Is Trust Vindicated?*
9. See Richard Butwell and Fred von der Mehden, "The 1960 Election in Burma," *Pacific Affairs*, XXXIII (June, 1960), 144-157.
10. Prior to the incorporation move, Burma's national police numbered more than 17,000. The Government's decision to absorb the S.P.R.'s into the

regular police would raise the figure to 44,000. *The Guardian* (Rangoon), May 25, 1960.

11. See *New York Times,* September 13, 1960.

12. There has recently been strong criticism of the D.S.I. by Burmese private businessmen because it allegedly enjoys various advantages in its competition with them (*The Nation,* July 4, 1960). See also Peter Simms, "The Facts Behind the D. S. I.," *The Guardian* (Rangoon), June 26, 1960, and "Burma's Army in Business, the DSI," *Far Eastern Economic Review* (March 17, 1960), pp. 587-589.

13. Brigadier Aung Gyi is the Central Council's Vice President and Colonel Maung Maung its General Secretary. The Vice President told N.S.A. district officers at a May meeting that the movement represented the foundation of democracy and that the N.S.A.'s should help district administrative officers in the discharge of their duties (*The Guardian* [Rangoon], May 30, 1960).

14. See Richard Butwell, "The New Political Outlook in Burma," *Far Eastern Survey,* February, 1960, pp. 21-27.

15. Premier Nu vowed in a press conference, however, that the frontier administration would never "degenerate" into a "military administration" (*The Guardian* [Rangoon], September 10, 1960).

16. For a description of Burmese Army personnel in Israel for this purpose, see Maung Maung, "Co-op and Communal Villages in Israel," *The Guardian* (Rangoon), June 29, 1960.

17. See U Nu, *The Pyidaungsu Policy* (Rangoon: "Clean" A.F.P.F.L., 1959).

18. Brigadier Aung Gyi declared at a mass rally of the N.S.A. in late 1959 that the preservation of democracy should be a main aim of the populace. *The Guardian* (Rangoon), November 2, 1959. See also the official document *Hawkers of Human Hope & We (Ideological Defense)* (Rangoon: Ministry of Defence, 1959).

19. It is interesting, however, that the Army has used Buddhism, the country's traditional religion, in its ideological struggle with the Communists. Its booklet *Dhamantaraya* (Rangoon: Ministries of Information and Defence, 1959) is a national best-seller.